SAANI BAAT

Other Books by Tijan M. Sallah

Poetry Collections
When Africa Was a Young Woman
Kora Land, Poems
Dreams of Dusty Roads: New Poems
Dream Kingdom: New and Selected Poems
Harrow: London Poems of Convalescence

Short Stories
Before the New Earth: African Short Stories

Biography
Chinua Achebe: Teacher of Light, A Biography

Ethnograpy:
Wolof: The Heritage Library of African Peoples

Poetry Anthologies (Edited)
New Poets of West Africa
The New African Poetry: An Anthology (coedited with Tanure Ojaide)
AWorld Assembly of Poets

SAANI BAAT

ASPECTS OF AFRICAN LITERATURE AND CULTURE
(Senegambian and other African Essays)

TIJAN M. SALLAH

AFRICA WORLD PRESS
TRENTON | LONDON | CAPE TOWN | NAIROBI | ADDIS ABABA | ASMARA | IBADAN | NEW DELHI

AFRICA WORLD PRESS
541 West Ingham Avenue | Suite B
Trenton, New Jersey 08638

Copyright © 2021 Tijan M. Sallah

All rights reserved. No part of this publication may be reproduced, stored in a retrieval system or transmitted in any form or by any means electronic, mechanical, photocopying, recording or otherwise without the prior written permission of the publisher.

Cover design: Ashraful Haque
Book design: Lemlem Tadesse

Library of Congress Cataloging-in-Publication Data

Names: Sallah, Tijan M., 1958- author.
Title: Saani baat : aspects of African literature and culture (Senegambian and other African essays) / Tijan M Sallah.
Description: Trenton : Africa World Press, 2021. | Includes bibliographical references and index. | Summary: "The title of this book of literary criticism Saani Baat: Aspects of African Literature and Culture, comes from the Wolof, Saani Baat, which literally means "to throw one's voice" in a conversation. In this rich and path-breaking collection of literary essays and criticism, the noted Gambian writer, Tijan M. Sallah, explores in provocative essays the theme of whether there is a Gambian national literature and how it differs from the literature of Senegal; explores the metaphysical systems and oratures of the Wolof and Jola peoples of Senegal and The Gambia; discusses the new Gambian poets and their poetry, and examines the writings and life of the late veteran Gambian writer, Lenrie Peters"-- Provided by publisher. Identifiers: LCCN 2020050579 | ISBN 9781569026977 (hardback) | ISBN 9781569026984 (paperback)
Subjects: LCSH: Gambian literature--History and criticism. | Gambian literature (English)--History and criticism. | Literature and society--Gambia. | American literature--African American authors--History and criticism.
Classification: LCC PR9378 .S25 2021 | DDC 820.9/96651--dc23
LC record available at https://lccn.loc.gov/2020050579

In Memory of Two Friends and Scholars on
Senegambia:
Professor Sulayman S. Nyang
Professor David P. Gamble

CONTENTS

Acknowledgments ix
Preface xi
Chapter 1. Dreams of Katchikali: The Challenge of a
    Gambian National Literature 1
Chapter 2. Senegambian Wolof Poetry 23
Chapter 3. Toward a Wolof Metaphysics and Philosophy:
    Some Preliminary Reflections 39
Chapter 4. Jola Verbal Arts of Senegambia: A Question In
    Search of a Literature 65
Chapter 5. The New Gambian Poets and Their Poetry 89
Chapter 6. To My Late Friend Dr. Lenrie Peters: The
    Gambian Vessel Emptied of Its Poetry 99
Chapter 7. Phillis Wheatley: A Brief Survey of the Life and
    Works of a Gambian Slave-Poet in New England
    America 111
Chapter 8. Harlem Renaissance: Thoughts on the
    Movement and On Its Poetry 125
Chapter 9. The Eagle's Vision: The Poetry of Tanure
    Ojaide 143
Chapter 10. An Entire Star Has Left Us: Chinua Achebe,
    In Memoriam 159
Glossary 171
Bibliography 177
Index 183

ACKNOWLEDGMENTS

I acknowledge, with gratitude, the following journals or publications where some of the essays in this book previously appeared: "The Eagles Vision: The Poetry of Tanure Ojaide," which appeared in *Research in African Literatures*. Vol. 26, no. 1 (Spring 1995); "Phillis Wheatley: A Brief Survey of the Life and Works of a Gambian Slave-Poet in New England America," which appeared in *Wasafiri*, University of Kent, Canterbury, no. 15 (Spring 1992): 27-31; "The New Gambian Poets and Their Poetry" which appeared in *Asymptote Journal* (Winter 2018), and "An Entire Star Has Left Us: Chinua Achebe, In Memoriam," which appeared in *Chinua Achebe: Tributes and Reflections*, edited by Nana Ayebia Clarke and James Currey, London, Ayebia Clarke Publishing. I also wish to thank the poets Tanure Ojaide, Mariama Khan, Bala Saho, and Momodou Sallah, for granting me copyright permission to quote from their poetry. Other poets and authors have been quoted for critical purposes under principles of fair use. Whereas every effort has been made to duly acknowledge and, where relevant, to secure permission for quoted works, any ones that I may have missed are regrettably unintended. The author regrets any imperfections in this book and welcomes queries, where applicable, so they can be addressed in future editions.

PREFACE

Despite a large body of works on African literary criticism, discourses on Senegambian literature in English are few—if not rare. I have titled this book, *Saani Baat* or "voice throwing" to capture that discerningly expressive tendency in Wolof discourse where an unnoticed member "throws" his voice colorfully in a conversation to get noticed. This book of criticism (primarily from a Senegambian angle) looks at Gambian, African, and African diaspora poetry and at other literary works and also addresses some cultural matters in those domains. The traditional poetics of two major Senegambian ethnic groups, the Wolof and the Jola, as well as their metaphysics and philosophy, are addressed in three essays.

The essays in this volume vary in scope and content. Some are thoroughly researched expositions, some are snippets of reflections, and some are eulogies. "Dreams of *Katchikali:* The Challenge of a Gambian National Literature" was delivered over twenty years ago as a provocative talk at a conference in Washington, DC, organized by Gambians, and wrestles with the question of a national literature in the context of a colonially imposed territory. Some of the ideas advanced in that essay appear now—on reflection—to be controversial. The chapter on "Senegambia Wolof Poetry" discusses different types of traditional Wolof poetics, and illustrates each type with specific examples. I drew heavily in that chapter from what I learned in my childhood from oral tradition; the essay includes my direct translation of oral traditional poems that possibly have never been recorded before. These oral traditions are widely shared in the Senegambia sub-region and have no known authorship.

Similar considerations also apply to my essay, "Towards a Wolof Metaphysics and Philosophy: Some Preliminary Reflections," which is a highly innovative and pioneering chapter which examines Wolof metaphysical concepts, such as space, time, values and issues associated with what it means to be human in the Wolof universe. I am hoping these pioneering essays will inspire scholars to dig deeper into our indigenous cultural systems. "Jola Verbal Arts of Senegambia: A Question in Search of a Literature," is also an equally pioneering essay on the orature of a little researched but important Senegambian marginalized ethnic group. The essay argues that the verbal marginalization of the Jola has come from their resistance to Euro-Christian westernization and Arabo-Islamic influences. "The New Gambian Poets and Their Poetry" is an appetizer (or brain teaser) on the new poetic voices that have been steadily making their mark on the Gambian literary scene. "To My Late Friend, Dr. Lenrie Peters: The Gambian Vessel Emptied of Its Poetry" is a eulogy for the "founding father" of Gambian literature and examines the paradoxes of his complex identity. The piece, "Phillis Wheatley: A Brief Survey of the Life and Works of a Gambian Slave-Poet in New England, America," reclaims her as a Senegambian poet and documents her remarkable life, as she faced the double jeopardy of blackness and femininity in chauvinistic, ante-bellum America. Surmounting overwhelming odds, Phillis became a living example of the genius of the "Negro" and the "founding mother" of African-American literature. "Harlem Renaissance: Thoughts on the Movement and Its Poetry" revisits the poetry of that vibrant black cultural nationalist movement, which continues to inspire black arts globally. The essay, "The Eagle's Vision," explores the poetry of Tanure Ojaide, one of Nigeria's foremost poets after the Okigbo/Soyinka generation, and discusses how the poet uses literary devices from his native Orhobo oral tradition to fight political corruption and tyranny. I wrote the essay in the early nineties, and it was one of the first pieces of criticism on this consequential poet, whose work has now spawned a vibrant critical industry in Nigeria. The piece, "An Entire Star Has Left

Us," is a eulogy for my friend Chinua Achebe, whose impact on the development of contemporary African literature is enduringly wide and deep.

These essays on Gambian and on other aspects of African literature are "voice throwings"—critical conversations on culture, literature and orature, that, I hope, will ignite discussions about why it is important to study and preserve our cultures. At a minimum, I want the essays to stimulate conversations among Senegambians and other Africans—about our cultural environment, to look at ourselves and at our narratives with intelligent curiosity. "Can anything good come out of The Gambia?" asked the Gambian writer Lenrie Peters. "Of course, of course," I respond. I urge the reader to enter these pages and discover what I mean.

--Tijan M. Sallah
Potomac, Maryland
August 20, 2020

CHAPTER 1

DREAMS OF KATCHIKALI: THE CHALLENGE OF A GAMBIAN NATIONAL LITERATURE

The question of a Gambian national literature, the search for a distinct narrative rooted in the sensibilities and rituals of a place, has been as illusive as the search for a Gambian national identity. What does it mean to be a Gambian; to be part of a population of about two million; to be dependent on a groundnuts or peanuts monocrop economy; to be geographically surrounded, except for the coastline, by Senegal; to be the confluence of some four major ethnic groups: Mandinka, Wolof/Serer, Fula/Tukolor, and Jola; to be defined spiritually by the predominant import of the religion of Islam mixed into a sumptuous syncretism with the folk beliefs of an atavistic past? What is it that ties this peculiar constellation of factors into some common identity? In a sense, the concept of The Gambia is purely a colonial construct; what distinguishes it from its neighboring Senegal, is fundamentally the experience of having been under a different colonial dispensation; more specifically the experience of surviving British *Indirect Rule* as opposed to French *Assimilation* cultural policy as was in Senegal. So, if The Gambians were today to cease speaking English or the Senegalese French and at the same time erase that anguished memory which is hidden in the manners, morals, and habits of thought and institutions so permeated by colonial inhibitions, then we would be speaking of a Senegambian culture. But this is an exercise in political fiction: the reality is that The Gambia is today an independent polity, has been evolving a distinct national culture, one so indelibly stamped with British superimposed sensibilities that to speak of Gambian culture involves speaking in the same universe as:

- Cricket (British game similar to baseball);
- Cable & Wireless (British-based telecommunications company);
- The Beatles (a sixties British rock band);
- The Twist (American-originated and British-popularized worldwide dance craze of the early sixties);
- Monopoly or Ludo (two British-popularized board games);
- Guiness (a British/Irish stout beer); Vermouth (a British fortified wine); Vimto (a purple fruity British soft drink);
- Rothman King Size; Piccadilly; Benson & Hedges (all British brand cigarettes);
- Custard (a British egg and cream mix sweet dessert);
- Cow & Gate (a British brand dairy product);
- Royal Victoria Hospital (British colonially built main hospital in The Gambia, named after Queen Victoria);
- William Shakespeare (the British dramatist); Geoffrey Chaucer (the British medieval poet) and George Orwell (British novelist and essayist);
- Stamps and currency with the posters of King George and Queen Elizabeth;
- Imperial nursery rhymes like "*John Bull-e*;"
- Empire Day (a holiday that used to be observed annually in The Gambia on the school day preceding Queen Victoria's birthday, May 24);
- "Rule, Britannia," (a British patriotic song);
- And, of course, that jingoistic chant for imperial hegemony, "God Save the Queen."

To speak, therefore, of a Gambian national literature, is to speak of that narrative which emerged with the colonial construction of a Gambian nation. It cannot be a literature narrowly confined within an ethnic text or context, though it could draw from that rich repository of folk repertoires; but it must intrinsically be a literature which, by virtue of the fact that English has become The Gambia's national lingua franca, must of necessity also be written in English. When ethnic texts have not broken parochial boundaries to permeate the understanding of other ethnic groups in The Gambian nation, they cannot be called national literature. Even Arabic, which is transethnic in its appeal in The Gambia, because it has been strictly limited to a religious milieu, has not risen to the status of the language of a national literature because Gambians who are animists or Christians, do not subscribe to its use and are therefore excluded from its advantage. I know I have advanced a controversial thesis that the definition of a national literature is one that uses a national language; in this sense, ethnic texts could perhaps qualify if they get translated in the English lingua franca that all Gambians have the freedom and in some cases the opportunity to learn and to use.[1]

I have deliberately titled this essay, "Dreams of Katchikali: The Challenge of a Gambian National Literature," to appeal to a shrine that is uniquely Gambian in character. Katchikali is a shrine in the Kombo Saint Mary Division with a pack of sacred crocodiles and an attending priest; Gambian nationals flock to it for prayer or for cures of various physical and spiritual ailments. As far as I know, no equivalent of Katchikali exists in Senegal, except perhaps in Casamance where the Jola ethnic group maintain primordial African belief systems, unsullied by the encroachment of Islam or Christianity. Not surprising, therefore, that The Gambian writer Lenrie Peters, that paterfamilias of a national Gambian literature in English, would have his second book of poems called *Katchikali* (1971). Was he directly conscious of the fact that he was forging a national literature? Was he aware of the fact that so much depends on the founding father of a national literature? In *Katchikali*, Peters's poem reads, "Can any good thing come/out of Gambia? /Wait./nay; go and see."[2] The lines suggest an intriguingly interrogatory self-doubt, but the answer, "go and see," point to the fact that some good coming out of The Gambia may not only be in the realm of possibility, but also probability. I will twist the poem and ask, "Are Gambians capable of producing a national literature?" Well, let us see in the next section.

Lenrie Peters and the Forging of National Literature

I have argued in the Gambian *Daily Observer* of 1993, as follows:

> Our literature in English is still young. Lenrie Peters is the pioneer. His novel, *The Second Round*, and his books of poetry, *Satellites* and *Katchikalli*, are well known, spanning themes of homecoming and the anxieties and frustrations of a "been-to" returning to an independent Africa. William Conton, a Gambian who has spent most of his life in Sierra Leone is sometimes identified with Gambian literature because of his novel, *The African*. /These literary pioneers, however, suffered one major syndrome: *cultural marginality*. By reason of upbringing, their interpretation of the Gambian universe is not significantly different from that of the African-American Alex Haley, author of *Roots*, or of the Afro-Caribbean Maryse Conde, author of *Segu*. The traditional sensibilities of the Senegalese Sembene Ousmane or the Nigerian Chinua Achebe eluded them.[3]

To understand Peters's writings, it is important to get a brief snapshot of his family background. Peters is quintessentially a Krio, which means that he is a descendant of liberated Africans.[4] According to Akintola Wyse, the name Krio may have been derived from the Yoruba *akiriyo*, which means "those who go about from place to place after church."[5] Perhaps this is a reference to the fact that Christianity is at the core of the Krio identity, for Europeans often used the Krio as a "buffer class" in between them and "native" Africans, and as conduits for the spread of Christian teachings and of Westernization in general. The experience of being a Krio suggests that Peters is an "uprooted" African. As such, he does not write out of any distinct African indigenous tradition. As Peters himself once put it at the Berlin Horizon Conference on World Cultures, "My family has been detribalized for nearly four generations. I am like Alex Haley. I am looking for my roots."⁶ The special experience of being a Krio, I would argue, has weaned Peters away from tribal or nativistic allegiances and therefore made him into an avowed Pan-Africanist. We should note that the strongest advocates of Pan-Africanism have been not traditional or indigenous Africans, but Africans at the margin of African indigenous cultures; more specifically, the Afro-Caribbean, the African-American, and the Krio or liberated African. The names that come to mind are Marcus Garvey, George Padmore, W. E. B. Du Bois, and Edward Wilmot Blyden. In short, Africa, as a totalizing construct, is the comfortable niche foremost of Africans with a reconstructed identity.

To be more specific about Peters's family background, he was born in Bathurst (now Banjul) on September 1, 1932, the son of Pa Lenrie Peters Sr., an accountant at the export-import company, S. Madi Ltd., and Auntie Keziah Peters, who came from a privileged family which boasted, among his brothers, the Maxwells, the first African graduates of Oxford University.⁷ Both parents immigrated to The Gambia from Sierra Leone. His hardworking father studied Greek and Latin at Fourah Bay College, and his mother was raised in England as a young girl in a Victorian family. The couple were Anglicans, and they met in The Gambia where they married and became one of the most respected families in the country. Peters's father also edited the private weekly newspaper, *The Gambia Echo*, while working as an accountant, and it may not be entirely wrong to assume that his mother, but especially his father, may have provided the environment and impetus for Peters's love of literature and writing. Peters was a middle child, boasting two older sisters, Bijou (a nurse and journalist); Florence Mahoney (a distinguished historian), and two younger sisters, Ruby (a retired UN administrator) and Alaba (now diseased, but a figure in film and big business). Peters's early education was at St. Mary's Primary School and at the Methodist Boys' High School in The Gambia. Because of the inadequacy of the science curriculum at the Methodist Boys' High because of laboratory facilities and qualified teachers, Peters was sent for a two-year science study at Prince of Wales High School in Freetown, Sierra, where he received his Higher School Certificate and from where, upon his return to The Gambia, he left for Cambridge Technical College in England, where he studied latin and physics. He proceeded, between 1953 and 1956, to study natural sciences at Trinity College, Cambridge, becoming president of the African Students' Union, after which he studied medicine at the University College Hospital, London.[8] In Cambridge, he began writing poetry and plays, became a Pan-Africanist, and started *The Second Round*, which was first published in 1965, under the Heinemann African Writers Series. While pursuing his versatile interests-- the scientist and the renaissance man-- Peters pursued broadcasting with the British Broadcasting Corporation (BBC) Africa Service and later moved to the World Service. In 1969, Peters returned home and, in 1972, after two years of government service at Bansang Hospital, went into a private partnership with Dr. Samuel J. Palmer, starting the first private clinic in The Gambia, the Westfield Clinic, located in Kanifing.[9]

In a sense Peters's own peculiar personal biography informs his own writings. His novel, *The Second Round*, is in many ways autobiographical, depicting as its protagonist, a certain Dr. Kawa, who returns to Sierra Leone after studies in England, but finds himself alienated from life in Freetown because of the uneasy mixture of traditional African living and the demands and time consciousness of the modern world he left behind in England. To borrow a metaphor from the Nigerian poet Gabriel Okara, life in Freetown was, in short, filled with the existential tensions characteristic of listening to the "piano and the drum."[10] The return of the "been-to" is made all the more frustrating by societal expectations: Kawa's mother is happy to see her son back and thanked the "English for giving her son knowledge and sophistication," but "lamented their neglect of his stomach."[11] So, like all good African mothers, she made her prime business the task of feeding her prodigal son well, compensating retroactively for his years of food deprivation as a student in England. Kawa's mother and friends expect him to get married, to settle down, and to acquire property, but Kawa's reluctance and restlessness eventually lands him into a betrayed friendship with Laura and into the unhappy lives of Marshall and his wife Clara. Eventually, Kawa leaves Freetown to search for an illusory contentment in some lonely provincial hospital. This novel is essentially author life-reflexive; it very much mirrors aspects of Peters's own life.

But autobiography worked into fiction does not necessarily make for bad literature. There are beautiful poetic lines in *The Second Round* and the book often echoes with moments of philosophizing about the condition of the black man. This often gives one the feeling of a writer who is overly self-conscious and who has a Pan-African cause, but it is a cause uninformed by a local traditional consciousness. In fact, the immediacy of the effects of the social realism is often filtered through the sieve of alienation, through the mental framework of an alienated African-- or should I not say, of an alienated Gambian, a Gambian not alienated from the physical reality of The Gambia, but from its centuries-tested traditional psychology, from its intergenerationally transmitted oratures. Consider these lines from Kawa responding to his mother, using his English-trained wisdom:

> But we mustn't spend the next century moaning about what they have done and what they have not done for us. Perhaps it's just as well they haven't done too much. At least we shall have less to undo before we restart. We must get on with tackling with the vital problems of Africa without making martyrs of ourselves. It's becoming a neurosis. I believe in Africa and I believe in the black man because he still has warmth left in him-- the same warmth you and I borrow from the sun and transmit to the earth. He still has a smell so that when you go into his house you know a human being has been there. It is a kind of identity.[12]

As much as the lines appear to be dismissive of whining against colonialism and celebrates self-responsibility in blackness and in Africanity, it conveys some self-defeatist aspects; for what self-apprehending African would take the smell in his house as a kind of identity? Or am I taking this biological imagery literally? Or was Peters simply carried away by the excesses of his pen? Of course, a tradition-conscious African has better sources for an identity. Also, is the African really any warmer than the European; is he intrinsically any different, except that he has been shaped by different historical and environmental factors? I do not believe so, but I know that some advocates of Negritude believe in some intrinsic difference.

Even the story that Peters develops in the latter chapters of the novel, equating the passive, vulnerable character of sea turtles to the situation of black Africans, does not borrow much from African oral traditions; it appears to be artificial and contrived, although lavishly rich with his poetic skills and with his knowledge of biology as a remarkably well-trained surgeon. When Peters notes the situation of seaturtles as the "dismal spectacle of a harmless creature worn out by the demands of survival and he, Man, had inflicted great suffering on her,"[13] is he drawing a parallel with the condition of black Africans? Peters asks some profound philosophical questions, "But what has death to do with suffering? Both are natural laws--indisputable."[14] But in that realm of nature, there is "no need for powerful muscles and large hearts."[15] What one needs is a "tiny speck of brain and a weapon" and the possibilities are in one's hand to "subjugate the whole world."[16]

I have delved in some brief detail into *The Second Round* because it is one of the first, if not the first novel written by a Gambian, though it can hardly be called a great model for a national literature from a tradition-conscious point of view. It has great writing in it, but great writing alone does not make for a great national novel. I have argued elsewhere that "in so far that the literary works of Gambians reflect the values, attitudes and beliefs of our society, the ideas and images we live by in our 'shared house,' there is a Gambian literature."[17] Does *The Second Round* meet that test? The Gambian reading public is to judge.

I wish to argue that the start of a Gambian national literature started with Peters's book of poems, *Katchikali*. Although in his first book of poems, *Satellites*, Peters meanders and philosophizes about various aspects of the African and human condition, but except for a few poems about homecoming and personal loss, there is hardly anything in the earlier works to merit being called Gambian literature. Of course, there is that beautiful poem of homecoming titled, "We Have Come Home," which deals with the hopes and anxieties of the "been to" set against the natural landscape of The Gambia:

> We have come home
> from the bloodless wars
> With sunken hearts
> Our boots full of pride
> From the true massacre of the soul
> When we have asked
> 'What does it cost
> To be loved and left alone'[18]

The student's return after being triumphant with his studies, the "bloodless wars," is marked by the uncertainties at home and the aspect that "the spinning coin" or "luck" plays in people's final destinies:

> We have come home
> When the dawn falters
> Singing songs of other lands
> The death march
> Violating our ears
> Knowing all our love and tears
> Determined by the spinning coin.
>
> We have come home
> To the green foothills
> To drink from the cup
> Of warm and mellow bird song
> To the hot beaches
> Where boats go out to sea
> Threshing the ocean's harvest
> And the hovering, plunging

Gliding gulls shower kisses on the waves.[19]

In much of Peters's poetry, there is a serious groping for self which manifests itself in the exploration of images from different traditions--African, European, American, and Asian-- and this self-search is sometimes intellectual, sometimes political, but always sincere. The poet's sophisticated musings bristle with names such as "Kafka," "Sunjiatta," "Samori," and "Socrates." But they remain at that level-- intellectual musings; the poet is rarely involved in these characters, either through a mastery of the related traditions or through strong instinctual identification. The poet remains largely coolheaded, aloof, almost like a scientist-poet-- lacking that passionate involvement which makes poetry more than just the product of intellectual labor, but also of social commitment and involvement. Compared to another Senegambian poet Leopold Sedar Senghor, there is a remarkable difference. Although both draw from the same general set of traditions or at least surrounded by them, Senghor, as a poet, deeply rooted in Serer traditions and in their gift of powers over the waters, shows more of a poetry of passionate involvement. But this is not to say that Peters is a better or worse poet; rather, this is to say that poets are products of a cultural and historical experience, and Peters, though sometimes not too satisfying to the local Gambian in his work, nevertheless remains sincere to his background.

But, except for the poem, "We Have Come Home," it is really in *Kachikali*, that Peters, the founding father, can be said to have returned home and started the forging of a national literature. In one of the poems in *Katchikali*, Peters uses incantatory rhythms and images to celebrate the Gambia River:

> A slender river flows
> three hundred miles to harbor;
> wide-mouthed towards the sun,
> down inguinal pursuit
> of open sea; tomorrow
> fenced by mangroves,
> settlements, ancient traditions,

The Gambia flows;
a trusting limb of elegance.[20]

In a sense, Peters's imagination is trapped within the traditions of European poetry, but in these lines and in many lines in *Katchikali*, he remains faithful to African (and for that matter Gambian) themes and images. As Chinua Achebe in his novel, *Anthills of the Savannah* (1987), refers humorously (or perhaps sarcastically) to Senghor as a "Manding-Gaul,"[21] Peters could also be referred to in Nathan Hare's terminology as an "Afro-Saxon." But Peters is an Afro-Saxon with a difference; he has pioneered our national literature. In the poem, "Katchikali," Peters takes us to the shrine that is truly Gambian:

> And the crocodiles
> of another world
> under your waters
> tame as pumpkins
> Katchikali
>
> Katchikali, Katchikali
> the women weight-drowned
> towards the farms bend
> their knees and say a prayer
> Katchikali[22]

And the respect the poet feels for this shrine of sacred crocodiles comes when he challenges Gambian's own neglect of their traditional heritage:

> and men strong as Baobabs
> press-ganged to clear your
> dense embraces
> the sweat of fear on their faces
> plead with every fateful stroke
> 'It is not I who destroys you
> it is not I Katchikali
> but those who ignore your mysteries.'[23]

At the end of the poem, the poet mourns the commercialization and defilement of the shrine, what the poet calls, "seething self-interest and corruption and the demon of gain in your waters Katchikali."[24]

I have argued implicitly that Peters is the founding father of our national literature, and that it is in his book of poems, *Katchikali*, that he truly "returns" home and starts the project of a national literature. However, I have also argued that the cultural marginalization that Peters feels as a Krio has often made him preoccupied with the larger issues of the continent than with the specific indigenous traditions of the Gambia. Our founding father writes out of the tradition of English poetry, partly a reflection of his education and partly a reflection of his personal background as an "Afro-Saxon." Our founding father is a great poet and a great novelist in terms of style, but the substance of his work often leaves a taste of a lost person in search of his ancestry and himself than one rooted in the bedrock of a specific indigenous Gambian tradition. It is perhaps this cultural marginalization which makes Peters a Pan-Africanist, attacking the injustices of history, conscious that the loss of his roots came about through Europe's project of African colonization and enslavement. We now move to the new generation of writers.

The Second Generation of Gambian Writers

With the launching of a national literary tradition, there was a need for continuity in contribution and in a deepening of talent. Since his return to The Gambia in 1971, Peters has been a catalyst for creative writing in the country, encouraging young writers and serving as founding editor of *Ndanaan*, the short-lived literary magazine published by the Gambian Writers Club between 1971 and 1976. I myself have benefited in the early 1970s, from his selfless encouragement and sacrifice in sparing his busy time as a medical doctor and seeing me in a spare room in the Westfield Clinic, reviewing my poetry and offering suggestions for improvement. The Welsh critic, Professor Stewart Brown, also acknowledges this catalytic role of Peters and also notes about *Ndanaan* and the emergence of a national literature:

> There were only five issues of Ndanaan, published intermittently over the five year period of its existence, and although occasional stories by Gambian writers appeared in other journals like *West Africa* in the 1970s and early 1980s, more than twenty years elapsed between the publication of Peters' novel, *The Second Round*, and the next significant work of prose fiction to be published by a Gambian author, Ebou Dibba's fine historical novel *Chaff on the Wind*, published in 1986. Since then, however, Dibba has published a second novel, *Fafa* (1989), and two young Gambians have published interesting collections of short stories: Nana Humasi (or Nana Grey-Johnson)'s *A Krio Engagement* (1987) and Tijan M. Sallah's *Before the New Earth* (1988). Sheriff Sarr's *Meet Me in Conakry* (1984), a work of popular fiction targeted at young adults but more widely read, has gone into its fifth edition in four years, and several Gambians have published poetry in international journals and anthologies.[25]

Brown is not very complimentary of the works published in *Ndanaan*, as he stated, "There is, in truth, no much that is intrinsically interesting in the material published in the journal (Ndanaan), except-- in terms of the argument of this essay-- that the themes touched by several of the writers reflect a growing awareness of-- and concern--for the history and particular political situation of The Gambia. Most pertinent is Gabriel J. Roberts's play, *A Coup Is Planned*, in Vol. 2., no. 1. of March 1972, which worries the issues of the power relationship between The Gambia and Senegal."[26] But should one denigrate a beginning, even if it may have been a false start; I would argue no. There was some merit to *Ndanaan* in that it provided a forum for any Gambian who had creativity in English to come out. The result is that many amateur writers like Swaebou Conarteh, Hassan Jagne, and Charles Jow first saw the light of day through *Ndanaan*. The Wolof have a saying that *Ku heep joodom waanyi dara jam* (He who belittles his origins diminishes his dignity);

therefore, we must respect *Ndanaan* as a literary event, if for no other reason than it was a beginning.[27]

But *Ndanaan* was not the only literary outlet for an emerging national literature; in the 1970s, Bemba Tambedou also started a program over Radio Gambia titled, *Writers of the Gambia*, to encourage amateur young writers and to give them national visibility. I personally got my first national exposure through this medium. In a very real sense, a national literature requires four important elements: a national language; a coterie of producers (writers); a constellation of intermediaries/dissemination platforms (publishers, magazines, book distributors, and libraries); and a critical mass of consumers (a reading public and critics). Among these elements must also emerge a culture of rewarding good literature so that young people can be inspired to tread on that path.

If one looks at factors which impede the development of a Gambian national literature, the biggest impediments have been the lack of a critical mass of readers with purchasing power, and the lack of a publishing and critics-industry. Much of the book publishing in The Gambia used to be done by the Government Printer and then this was followed by the Gambia Book Production and Material Resources Unit. Some of the luckier writers published internationally with Heinemann Publishing, Macmillan Publishers, or Three Continents Press. But, on the whole, most budding writers have problems finding publishing outlets for their works. As for book distributors, the scene is dismal. There are only two competent bookstores: Methodist Bookshop on Buckle Street, Banjul, and Chaaka's Bookshop on Clarkson Street, as well as a few bookshops in the high schools stocking curricula material that is not available to the larger public. Recently, Timbooktoo Bookshop on Bakau Newtown Road has emerged as a robust world-class bookshop, stocking books and other educational material outside the usual textbooks used in schools. It is one of the shining educational lights in the country. In terms of libraries, there is the National Library and the British Council Library, and the various high schools also maintain slim book collections. On the reading side, the reading public is usually confined to the high-schooled populace or high school students who have particular texts as required reading in their curricula or syllabi. This is a sad commentary, but a national literary culture cannot thrive only if reading is done if it is assigned and enforced through school curricula. Writers need to write literature that is relevant, and literacy needs to be democratized so that the pursuit of enlightening the mind through books is made into an intrinsic good of itself. Democratization of literacy, of course, requires a seriously committed government, which has been lacking in The Gambia.

The late Dr. Jabez Ayo Langley, former head of The Gambia civil service under President Dawda Kairaba Jawara, and a renowned expert on Pan-Africanism, mockingly told me of the government's lack of interest in literacy and literature as exemplified in the usually mindless content of the *Gambia News Bulletin*, the official organ of the government. He notes that the public enthusiasm for the paper is shown in the fact that they use it to wrap *gerte saaf* (roasted peanuts) or *nyambeeh nyebeh* and *diwteer* (cassava and palm oil), or sometimes even use it as toilet paper before they wash their hands with *kamalik* (soap). I note this to be part of what I have always noted as the Fogni syndrome, a tendency for retrogressive governments to keep their populations illiterate, hungry, and pregnant and to breed weaknesses in their citizenry so that they can continue their retrogressive rule.

But our national intellectual direction need not be this way. In fact, The Gambia has been developing a serious and able group of creative writers and a similar group of critical scholars. For the latter, I would mention the Gambian professor Mbye Cham (who is a leading authority on African film and who writes more on Senegalese film and fiction); Dr. Siga Jagne, who is the first professional Gambian critic to take seriously Mariama Ba and Tijan M. Sallah's works; the Nigerian professor Pamela J. Olubunmi Smith, who writes about the fictional works of Ebou Dibba; and the Jewish American scholar-critic, professor Samuel Garren and the Nigerian critic, professor Ezenwa-Ohaeto, who have critically written about Sallah's works and the Welsh professor Stewart Brown, who has been the most ardent champion-critic of an emergent Gambian national literature.

Among the new generation forging a Gambian national literature are Ebou Dibba (who has published three novels, *Chaff in the Wind*,1986; *Fafa*, 1989; and *Alhaji*, 1992-- the last which is a novel for young adults); Tijan M. Sallah (who has published eight books-- three books of poetry: *When Africa Was a Young Woman*, 1980; *Kora Land*, 1989; *Dreams of Dusty Roads*, 1993; one book of short stories, *Before the New Earth: African Short Stories*,1988; as well as two anthologies, *New Poets of West Africa, 1995*, and *The New African Poetry-- An Anthology, 1999*; and an ethnography, *Wolof* ,1996); Nana Grey-Johnson (who has published a book of short stories, *A Krio Engagement*, 1987, and most recently published two novels,*The Magic Calabash*, 1998 and *I of Ebony*, 1997, and another collection of short stories, *Children of the Spyglass*, 1996); Sheriff Sarr (who has published a juvenile travelogue, *Meet Me in Conakry*,1984); and Gabriel J. Roberts (who published a collection of plays broadcast over BBC, *Nine Plays for Radio*, 1973). There are other amateur writers such as Swaebou Conarteh (who has published two chapbooks of poetry, *Great Wrinkles Up the Sky's Sleeve*, 1981 and *Blind Destiny*, 1982); Bala S. K. Saho (who has published a mini-novel titled, *The Road to My Village*, 1994); Sally Singhateh (who has published a short novel for young readers titled, *Christie's Crisis*, 1998); and Modu F. Singhateh (who has published a collection of stories titled, *A Day in Their Lives*, 1984). These writers include most of the major ethnic groups of The Gambia. Dibba's father is Mandinka and his mother is Wolof; Sallah's father is Tukolor and his mother is Serer/Wolof; Grey-Johnson's father is Krio and his mother is Wolof; Sarr's father is Serer and his mother is Wolof; and Swaebou Conarteh, B.S.K. Saho, and S. Singhateh, M Singhateh have parents who are both Mandinka. The Gambia has yet to produce a writer who writes out of the Jola tradition.

Overall, it is refreshing to see the multiethnic identity of most of these writers, perhaps a fusion encouraged by the predominant and transethnic culture of Islam which emphasizes the faith rather than the ethnicity, unless the two become coincidental. Many of the writers, being products of interethnic marriages, point to the forging of a common Gambian culture-- not based on ethnic entrenchment or on ethno-nativist strategies of dominance-- but on unifying what is valuable from each ethnic group, emphasizing cultural unity. My friend and compatriot Professor Sulayman Nyang speaks of the *"Wol-Mande-Fulbeh"* civilization, referring to the cultural affinities and unity of the Wolof, Mandinka, and Fula civilizations; I would stretch this integrative paradigm to include the many "acephalous" and numerically minor ethnic groups of the Senegambia area, which include the Jola, Conyagi, Baynunka, Mandiago, and Pelpel, which I will subsume, though inaccurately, under the instrumental but unsatisfactory rubric of "Jola." This way, I will modify Nyang's paradigm for our subregion as the *"Wol-Mande-Fulbeh-Jol"* civilization, a more inclusive and accurate representation.

Among the new generation of writers, Dibba's *Chaff on the Wind* can be described as The Gambia's truly first national novel. Unlike Peters, Dibba writes out of England in voluntary self-exile. *Chaff on the Wind* is set in The Gambia of the 1930s, just before the Second World War. It details the story of two young men-- Dinding, a teenage Mandinka boy from a strict Muslim family, from upriver (provinces) who came to the colonial capital, Bathurst, to search for his fortunes. The other young man is Pateh, of Fula and *Cheddo* (pagan) origin, who also left rural areas for the capital in search of opportunity. Dinding, in particular, is drawn away from the life that his family has hoped for. Both young men got involved with a trader in highly profitable smuggling. Dinding, the sober and diligent Muslim, turns into a prosperous merchant smuggling goods into Senegal against war-time regulations, and Pateh, the wild hedonistic pagan, get entangled with him such that their two fates and tied destinies become "chaff on the wind" of circumstances. *Chaff on the Wind* is brilliant in the way in which it details village and urban life, the attitudes of various ethnic groups, and individual struggles with destiny.

Take the following passage from *Chaff in the Wind* which develops Dinding's interaction with Njartigeh (literally meaning in Wolof, the hospitable host) and the transformation of Dinding from a naive provincial boy, into what the novelist Dibba describes as "a young man with authority stamped on him":[28]

> "The marabou has asked me to tell you that if you want the special prayer he reserves only for those able to afford it, the *Listiharr*, then he will require some money."
> "Why should he want a *Listiharr* when he has nothing to show for several months here?" Dinding asked sharply.
> "I know how you feel. But the *Listiharr* is something special."
> "Yes, at a special price too, I bet."
> If anybody had told Njartigeth that such hardness could be instilled in anybody in such a short time, he would not have believed it. There was no doubt, it was going to be difficult to pull a fast one over the young man.
> "But do you know what is involved in the *Listiharr*?"
> "No, but I know you'll tell me."
> "The marabou has to live in isolation for a few days to be in a state of purity, purity of mind, and purity of spirit. That means he has to eat special food, mainly meat, so you see, that costs."
> "Njartigeh, enough is enough. What guarantee is there that this *Listiharr* will work any better than what he has already done?"
> "One does not lay odds on requests to God."[29]

This exchange, one of the most poignant in the novel, questions the mystification which pervades in the synchretic (Islam mixed with folk beliefs) culture of the Gambia. Dibba appears to be poking fun at the commercial and exploitative nature of Islam in The Gambia, the seemingly empty promises of faith healing; but he himself, unwittingly, becomes the victim of a materialist interpretation of a mystical relationship. Do we really understand the spiritual powers of marabous or should we just rule them all out as just fake? How do we explain similar behavior on the part of American presidents and their wives (e.g., recall Ronald and

Nancy Reagan who often sought advice from a psychic-astrologer, Nancy Quigley!). Is it totally unreasonable when heads of states consult and get executive council from spiritual figures, psychics, shamanists, or palm readers? Recall the cases of Ghana's first premier, Kwame Nkrumah and Yugoslavia's leader, Marshall Tito, who were alleged to follow the spiritual advice of a Senegalese Marabou, Cheikh Ibrahima Niasse (or Barham) of Kaolack, Senegal!

In the genre of poetry and, at the risk of being accused of being self-indulgent, my own poetic works have sought to forge a modern national poetic tradition. In my book of poems, *Kora Land*, I have sought to capture the Gambian landscape, its flora and fauna, and its traditional sensibilities into collective celebrations of place and memory. Take the poem, "Banjul Afternoon," which opens:

> The afternoon was hot.
> The river-breeze enveloped the city.
> We walked along Independence Drive,
> Staring at the Royal Victoria Hospital,
> And then the Texaco gas station.[30]

Later the poem continues:

> At McCarthy Square, facing the
> Imposing monuments, the clock tower,
> And the Quadrangle, the smell
> Of sweaty shoes arrested us.[31]

The foul smell of sweaty shoes known in Wolof as *kamambay* is a much derided (but also talked about) smell in Gambian folklore. The poem continues to celebrate the images of that colonial capital with these lines:

> Wolof women passed us,
> Dignified as ostrich,
> Chewing sticks in their mouths.
> Handbags strapped around their arms.

They spat at every corner,
Trading happiness for hygiene[32]

In a sense, the second generation of writers of The Gambia are forging a remarkably valuable tradition. They are pursuing meanings and ways to celebrate or to artistically dissect place, memory, and hope but, in doing so, they do not mind being irreverent. There is a sense in which their works make us confront the human condition in The Gambia in a way that has never been explored before: whether in Dibba's existential exploration of rural youths on escapades in the city as mere *Chaff in the Wind*, or in Sallah's celebration of place in *Kora Land*, or in Grey-Johnson's exploration of realistic lives in poignant narratives in *A Krio Engagement*. There is a mainstay that is distinctively Gambian in these works and that shows great promise in laying the foundation of a grand architecture for the forging of a national literature and consciousness.

Notes

1 I know the language question is complex. We, of course, need to promote the development of African languages for both problem solving and creative expression; otherwise, they risk being demoted to the status of junior partners in our communication toolbox or even may be made to atrophy. We need to encourage the growth of African languages because they are our children's first language, their native language and, through it, we can circumvent the inhibitions from using a foreign tongue and enable the easy assimilation of modern artistic and scientific habits of thought. I am, however, not naive to believe that all African languages need to be heavily invested in; some languages are just not economically and socially viable. For a language to survive, it needs to have a sufficient critical mass of users (speakers and/or writers). Also, using an African language often involves uneasy or unpleasant political bargaining within a given African polity; whose language do you use? The language of the majority, or of the plurality, or of the powerful (economically or politically) or of some combination of the three? Whose ethnic language would you promote as the national language? It is for this reason that I side with Chinua Achebe. Africans should write in whatever language they are comfortable with. If a person can write in their mother tongue, all the more for the better. Where colonial languages have served us well as a unifying national lingua franca, I do not see any reason why they

should not serve as a national language as long as they are employed in the service of African interests and sensibilities. In regions like East Africa, where a hybrid African language—Swahili, has served that constructive unifying role; well, that is for the better.

2. Lenrie Peters, "Poem 30," in *Selected Poetry* (London: Heinemann Educational Books, 1981), 47.
3. Tijan M. Sallah, "Words or Rice? The State of Literature in The Gambia," *Daily Observer*, October 8, 1993, 7.
4. I recognize the fact that I have made so much of Peters's Krio background, but there seems to be no other way of understanding his writings. I also recognize the fact that not all Krio are alike and can be pigeon-holed into one controversial category called liberated Africans. Krios vary in their degree of consciousness and identification with traditional African culture. Some Krio were part of the black poor in London who immigrated to Freetown, Sierra Leone; some were freed African slaves from Nova Scotia, Canada; some were runaway slaves or Cimarrons or Maroons, many of whom were Koromantee from the Gold Coast, and some were liberated Africans, mostly Yoruba, and a good number were Moslems, and are known as Moslem Krios or as Aku Marabouts.
5. Akintola Wyse, *The Krio of Sierra Leone: An Interpretive History* (Washington DC: Howard University Press, 1991): 6.
6. Al Imfeld, Horizon 1979 first Festival of World Culture, Transcription, Portraits of African Writers: Lenrie Peters (Berlin: Deutsche Welle, 1979): 3.
7. Pamela Roberts, *Black Oxford: The Untold Stories of Oxford University's Black Scholars* (Oxford: Signal Books, 2013): 62.
8. David Perfect, *Historical Dictionary of The Gambia, Fifth Edition* (Lanham: Rowman and Littlefield, 2016): 342-3.
9. Kwame Arko, "Protean Thou Shalt Be—Profile," *West Africa* 23 (December- January 5,1997), 2018.
10. Gerald Moore and Ulli Beier, *Modern Poetry from Africa* (Hammondsworth: Penguin Books, 1965): 93.
11. Peters, *The Second Round* (London: Heinemann Educational Books, 1975): 19.
12. Ibid., 23.
13. Lenrie Peters, *The Second Round* (London: Heinemann Educational Books, 1979): 111.
14. Ibid.
15. Ibid.
16. Ibid., 111.
17. Sallah, "Words or Rice?": 7.
18. Peters, *Selected Poetry*, 22.
19. Ibid., 23.
20. Ibid., 46.

21 Chinua Achebe, *Anthills of the Savannah* (New York: Anchor Books, 1988): 35.
22 Peters, *Selected Poetry*, 74.
23 Ibid.,75.
24 Ibid.
25 Stewart Brown, "Gambia Fictions," *Wasafiri* (Spring 1992), no. 15, 4.
26 Ibid.
27 Ibid.
28 Ebou Dibba, *Chaff in the Wind* (London: Macmillan Publishers, 1986): 159.
29 Ibid., 159-60.
30 Sallah, *Kora Land* (Washington, DC: Three Continents Press, 1989), 23.
31 Ibid.
32 Ibid.

CHAPTER 2

SENEGAMBIAN WOLOF POETRY

The proposition that Wolof orature is as profusely rich as the "Wolof mind" begs the question as to whether there is such a thing as a "group mind" in the same way that one could discuss an individual's "head" as a unified biological locus of thought capable of demonstrable rationality and consistency. One could speak of the Wolof mind as an archetypal construct based on the collation of thoughts, practices, values, and beliefs which brings together the Wolof as a self-cohering collectivity. The Wolof genius is in how the Wolof mind uses words, whether perfunctorily or carefully, as banter or to tell a story. The three dominant forms of Wolof orature are the story (*leb*), the proverb (*lebaatu*), and the poem (which manifests in a variety of forms discussed in the following section; the *woi* or "song" being the dominant form). The following discussion concentrates on Wolof poetry, examining different poetic forms as well as providing examples. Also discussed is the dynamic interaction between poetry as a verbal genre and society, as the nurturing context which gives rise to its creation and appreciation. Poetry, therefore, is an aesthetic mode of individual and social reflection and engagement.

A discussion of Wolof poetry must start with the question: Who are the Wolofs? The Wolof are principally a Senegambian people whose empire once spanned the states of Waalo, Kayor, Jolof, Baol, Siin, and Saalum in present-day Senegal and in The Gambia (an area I will refer to as Senegambia). Siin and Saalum were originally Serer states, but were later conquered by the Wolof and transformed by their influence. The Wolof speak of themselves as either "Wolof" or "Olof," but others refer to them as Jolof, a reference to one of its precolonial states. The Senegalese scientist and Egyptologist Cheikh Anta Diop, argues in his book, *Nations Negres et Culture* and traces the origin of many of the Wolof clans to the Nile basin. Today, the Wolof occupy roughly the same area as they did in the fifteenth century when they were described in the writings of the Portuguese explorer Alvise Cadamosto.[1]

There are essentially four types of Wolof poetic forms that warrant attention: *woi, taga, baaku,* and *kassak.* Differentiation between the forms is linked to social function and to context. The *woi* or "song" is the most popular and common of the poetic forms and is encountered on many levels: in evening storytelling or in *leb* when an elder attracts a herd of youths at his feet; in ceremonious occasions when there is communal drumming or *sabarr;* or in private expressions of happiness or boredom-relief, such as when a young girl pounds grain with pestle and mortar, or cooks or washes clothes or entertains friends. The *woi* often has a context: the *woi kat* or "singer" responds to the circumstance of joy or aspires or is induced to joy, or expresses the reverse mood of grief. The *woi* includes lullabies, funeral dirges, folk ballads, and ribald songs; the *woi kat* must be spurred to song by some feeling, even if is just merely the feeling of anticipation of a loved one's coming.

One of the most popular "old songs" or *woi* among the Wolof is a lullaby rich with historical significance. It goes:

> *Papa Malamin, sering dara,*
> *Bindal ma chi tee re.*
> *Tee re yoombul chi Saloum,*
> *Te Saloum nyaarri neg la.*
>
> *Nye teel bi waing la,*
> *Te waing bi waingi burr la.*
> *Burba burri Saloum la.*
> *Ayo Ayai ya,*
> *Ayo Ne ne,*
> *Ne ne Tuuti.*

Translated as:

Father Malamin, religious teacher (i.e., marabout*),
Write me a talisman.
Talismans are not easy to find in Saloum
For Saloum has just two rooms.

The third room is only a kitchen,
And that kitchen belongs to the king.
That king is the King of Saloum.
Ayo Ayai ya,
Ayo Baby,
Little Baby.[2]

This song, like many English nursery rhymes, is a coded way of representing events and issues that could not be openly discussed. The message of the song refers to the fourteenth century when the Kingdom of Saloum in Senegal was divided into two warring households-- converts to the newly introduced religion of Islam and adherents to the traditional old Wolof religion. An anonymous Senegalese scholar provides further insights about the lullaby:

> The "kitchen" mentioned in the song symbolizes the wives of the king-- particularly his fifth wife, an older woman captured in war. She retained her belief in the Wolof religion, and so did King of Saloum. The words of this Wolof lullaby refer to events, heroes, customs, beliefs and social structures that existed five centuries ago. They mark a particular moment in Senegal's long history of kingdoms, empires, long-distance trade, and continuous cultural contact. The influence of these institutions is still to be found in the multilayered and multifaceted cultures that exist in Senegal today.[3]

One must underscore this by noting that the message of the lullaby has great contemporary significance. As it was a social commentary then, it sheds great light on the received tension between contemporary bearers of the banners of the "cross" and "crescent," on the one hand, and those of the bearers of the "animistic" past. Although most Wolof have largely become followers of the Abrahamic faiths, the tendency to wear charms, jujus, or other methods of withdrawal to an animistic past is still ubiquitous and provides a "default option" whenever there are doubts about the Abrahamic sky.

The *woi* can sometimes take the form of an elegy, invoking both nostalgia and catharsis. Consider *Samba Njai ya baakh hon* or "Samba Njai was a good person," a *woi* celebrating, albeit posthumously, the "good" name and character of Njai:

Samba Njai ya baakh hon
Borom nyeti hol
Samba Njai boomu dee yeh
Toubab yüy joy

Translated as:

Samba Njai was so good,
The man with three-hearts.
When Samba Njai died,
Even the Europeans mourned
(Translated by author from oral tradition)

This *woi* has many facets to it: (1) the goodness of Njai is praised so that it remains in the collective communal psyche, so that the young can learn that good deeds fetch communal recognition and rewards; (2) the reference to "Europeans" is a hyperbole, suggesting that the death of Njai evoked sympathy even from "strangers" or from "outsiders" to the African cultural universe; and (3) the symbolic reference to "three-hearts" locates with jusfiable exaggeration the "goodness" and kindness of Njai where it really matters. This particular *woi* is often sang to the accompaniment of a *ndonki ndong*, a "small lead-drum" often trapped in the armpit of a lead-drummer, endowed with the polyphonic gymnastics of a talking drum.

The second most popular Wolof poetic form is the *taga* or "praise-poetry," which is rooted in the use of devices of flattery aimed at undermining even the most stoic of characters. In a *taga*, the oral poet evokes images to capture the senses of the one being praised, appeals to history and myth, and may even refurbish them in a favorable light just to win the nerves and heart of the subject of praise. In traditional Wolof society, "praise-poetry" was targeted at two classes of people--the *burr* (king) and the *gerr* (nobility). In a *taga* the praise-giver attempts to move the praise-recipient to a pleasure-frenzy so that the latter, in a heightened mood of pleasure and pride, is induced to increase his material rewards or tips (i.e., money and clothes) to the former. There are two sides to a *taga*, represented by the *taga kat* or by the *keye taga* (praise-singer) and by the *ki nu y taga* (praise-recipient), often locked in an interactive relationship of mutual regard.

Taga or "praise-poetry" was not an open trade for entry by every member of traditional Wolof society. One had to be a member of the griot caste; that is, the caste of the *gewel*, to practice the trade. The *gewel*, though considered members of a low caste in Wolof society, had a special place and role in the community. Not only did they have nurtured prowess in reciting praises and in narrating from memory the genealogies of noble families through ornate language, but they often performed the role of social or community healing through their remarkable gift of words and mastery of family lineage. David P. Gamble, the renowned British (turned- American) anthropologist on Senegambia, explains the social significance of the *gewel*:

> The "*gewel*" comprise different types of musicians and praisers. The more important families are attached to various high-ranking freeborn lineages, for whom they are the historians, memorizing the family genealogies, and being called on for information when the question of succession is being decided. They also act as town criers, relaying information from the village head or chief. At all major ceremonies, namings, circumcisions, marriages, burials, they play important roles, being rewarded on such occasions with generous gifts by their patrons. A person of high rank is obliged to make gifts to those below him or her, while the "*gewel*" has the right to claim them, and can shame publicly those who fail to show their generosity.[4]

In earlier days, every *ger* or "noble" or *burr* (king) kept a *gewel*, who was not only just an entertainer, but a close confidant or intimate counselor.

The caste system in Wolof society requires an explanatory detour. It is a by-product of the received rigidities of history, an opportunistic awareness of ancestory which confers benefits to individuals by a simple appeal to blood. Ascriptive status based on lineage determined who fitted on the top of the social ladder and who fitted on the bottom. Social stratification along a relatively rigid caste system (though not as rigid and inhumane as that of the Indian Hindu) ensued in a relatively "superior" and "inferior" caste. The *ger* (noble) or "superior" caste consisted of the *burr* (king), the *linger* (queen, princess), the *jambur* (freeborn), the *gor* (free person with usufruct rights),[5] and the *badola* (peasant, ordinary poor). Similarly, the *nyenyo* or "inferior" caste consisted of persons organized along artisanal trades: the *ude* (leatherworkers), the *tega* (goldsmiths, blacksmiths, silversmiths), the *gewel* (praise-singers, musicians), the *raba kat* (weavers), and the *eta kat* (wood carvers). According to Cheikh Anta Diop, it was not "rare for members of the lower caste to refuse to enter into conjugal relations with those of the higher caste, even though the reverse would seem normal."[6]

Whereas in many traditional societies stratification along caste lines benefits the upper caste to the detriment of the lower, the reverse appears to hold true in the case of the Wolof. Members of the lower caste reaped great material benefits from their superiors-- the latter being perpetually compelled to save face before their *nyenyo* (or *neno*) through patronage of the former's services. Diop explains:

> But--and herein lay the real originality of the system-- unlike the attitude of the nobles toward the bourgeoisie, the lords towards the serfs, or the Brahmans toward the other Indian castes, the ger could not materially exploit the lower castes without losing face in the eyes of others, as well as their own. On the contrary, they were obliged to assist lower caste members in every way possible; even if less wealthy, they had to "give" to a man of lower caste if so requested. In exchange, the latter had to allow them social precedence.[7]

In a sense, the ruling behavioral motivation of the nobles before their *nyenyo* or, more specifically, their *gewel*, was commitment to the virtue of *jom* (dignity or integrity), which determined social acceptability.

Wolof poetics is intimately linked to the propagation of socially redeeming cultural values. In this sense, there are certain predominant sets of virtues which characterize Wolof society and which conditions individual behavior and features universally in the Wolof poetic repertoire. Virtues such as:

- *jom* (self-dignity or personal integrity),
- *teranga* (hospitality or generous predisposition toward visitors-guests-strangers),
- *moun* (patience),
- *rafet* (beauty, goodness),
- *dega* (truth-telling),
- *baakh* (goodness),
- *set* (personal cleanliness),
- *ngom* (faith in elders and in spiritual forces),
- *fula* (dignified self-consciousness),
- *faida* (self-willing, assertive self-respect),
- *ham ham* (knowledge, wisdom),
- *tegin* (good manner, good etiquette),
- *kersa* (respectable predisposition towards others),
- *yaru* (discipline), and
- *man man* (personal skill)

are highly desirable qualities which confer significant respect to those who possess or exhibit them.

In a typical *taga* the appeal to these virtues is often accompanied by deliberate exaggeration. But in a *woi* the *woi-kat* (singer) may be more levelheaded as the intent of the art is not just in immediate remuneration. The *baaku* (praise-challenge poem) represents a poetic form closely related to the *taga*. The *baaku* is an adversarial poetic form which features in the context of a competition where there are clear opposing sides. It is encountered during periods of war when it is used to fire the mettle of warriors or in wrestling matches when it is used to stir the spirit of a star-wrestler. In a *baaku*, the heroic is invoked and praises are heaped on the chosen hero in order to boost his morale and confidence and to tilt the odds in favor of his victory. In the Gambian town of Serekunda, one of the most famous *baaku* was that dedicated to Bala, a local hero-wrestler of the 1960s and 1970s, who demonstrated extraordinary wrestling prowess. Bala was not unlike Chinua Achebe's protagonist in *Things Fall Apart* (1969)- the celebrated Obi Okonkwo who "was slippery as a fish in water. Every nerve and every muscle stood out on [his] arms, on [his] back and [his] thigh, and one almost heard them stretching to breaking point."[8]

The *baaku* for Bala influenced even the youngest of kids in Serekunda who would be heard singing occasionally on the playground:

Denku, denku
Denku, denku, denku
Bala mo ko dan nel
Cham! denku, denku
Denku, denku, denku

Peul-bi mo ko dan nel
Cham! denku, denku
Denku, denku, denku

Translated as:

Denku, denku
Denku, denku, denku
Bala fell him down.
Alas! *denku, denku*
Denku, denku, denku

The Peul (i.e., Fula) fell him down.
Alas! *denku, denku*
Denku, denku, denku.
  (Translation by author from oral tradition)

Denku is essentially an onomatopoeia utilized as a sonorous complement to drumbeats accompanying a hero-wrestler. The hero here, Bala, is praised for having defeated many great local wrestlers, including the once invincible MaSanneh, a Jola of Foni, who was the inspirational pride of his village and people. The Wolof term *cham* used in the "praise-challenge," is an invigorating exclamatory device, often intended to rejuvenate the spirit of the praised hero. The ethnic reference to the "Peul" or the "Fula" as having defeated the "Jola," is a succinct illustration of the type of relationship which the Wolof refer to as *kal* or "traditional joking relationships between individuals or ethnic groups."

A typical wrestling match where *baaku* was widely used, was the *lamba*, a wrestling tradition peculiar to the Serer ethnic group but which has become a "tournament game" associated with harvest celebrations all over Senegal. *Lamba* literally means "touching"--the suggestion being that the wrestler deals with his opponent by "feeling" or by exploring the rival's strength through exploratory touching. In a *lamba* contest, the object of a wrestler is to force his opponent to lose balance so that his body touches the ground. *Lamba* competitions take place annually in the regions of Sine and Saloum in Senegal (regions, as noted earlier, significantly altered by Wolof influence) during the period after a crop harvest or sometimes before the first planting of crops. [9] Hero-wrestlers represent their villages in bouts of competition and, often, the wrestlers consult with their marabouts to get *terre* (juju) and *saa fara* (protective magic potions) and would be accompanied by drummers, village fans, and other supporters reciting a *baaku*, telling of their hero's invincibility and prowess.

The final Wolof poetic form that requires attention is the *kassak*, which is uniquely associated with circumcision. D. P. Gamble describes succinctly circumcision culture:

> The boys are escorted out of the village in the early morning for circumcision.... They are then taken to an enclosure where they stay until their wounds are healed. ...They wear traditional garments of locally woven cotton cloth and pointed caps. Each boy has as his constant companion an older youth, if possible, a cross-cousin who looks after him and attends to his needs. The boys are taught special circumcision songs (*kasak*) and their significance, learn how to communicate with each other by

means of secret signs (*pasin*), and are given instruction about correct adult behavior and sexual matters, as well as learning from the general process of strict discipline. The initiation process is a typical "rite of passage", setting those who were carefree children on the path to adulthood and responsible behavior. Once the boys are able to move around freely, then they have the right to chase any woman or girl they encounter.[10]

The enclosure (or more appropriately shelter) that Gamble refers to is called by the Wolof *mbaar*. The concept *mbaar* has no easy English equivalent; it may perhaps be more correctly translated as a "processing shop" or as a "miniature cosmos/world," where rough, uncircumcised boys (*aat*) are transformed into sexually aware and responsible adults. The personalities of the *mbaar* consist of the *njuli* (the newly circumcised), the *salbeh* (guardians-assistants of the *mbaar*), the *botal mbaar* (the big brother or custodian of the *mbaar*), the *kumakh* (the spiritual protector), and the *ngamaan mbaar* (the doctor). Among the newly circumcised, there is further differentiation within the *mbaar* according to age-seniority. The youngest among the circumcised, because of being the closest to being a baby, is referred to as the *tohal mbaar* (derived from the Wolof *tohental* meaning "sperm" or "water" or "source of life"); he is followed consecutively by the *goli mbaar*, the *lichen mbaar* and so on, up to the oldest of the newly circumcised who is called *habaan mbaar*.[11]

In a typical *mbaar* recitation of the *kassak*, as a poetic form, is often performed loudly, usually with a lead poet chanting some lines followed by the response of the newly circumcised. The "call and response" pattern of poetic recitation, being a highly participatory poetic form, dominates in a *kassak*.[12] Consider the following:

Jel na lengeh nyef ko njuli njai tak

Translated as:

I take the cane and spanked the newly circumcised
(Translated by author from oral tradition)

This call by the "lead poet" who is often *salbeh*, is followed by a response by the *njulis*:

Naar ya tak na mbaar tak;

Translated as:

The moor (i.e., *naar*) has flown and landed on the *mbaar*.
(Translated by author from oral tradition)

The "call-response" pattern may last for a long period followed by variations, and often impromptu switches to other *kassaks* without any pause or break.

One of the most popular *kassaks* which every *njuli* must know, is the primer, *Taguna mbaar njai*, or "I waved bye to the *mbarr njai*"— with the *mbaar* given the prototype Wolof last name, Njai. The *kassak* goes:

Taggu naa mbaar njai
Taggoo tuma mbaar njai
Singa joli Maa faal
Tingara tingara loo
Tei ma feili mbaar
Man feiwaii lengee
Feiyatu ma lengee
Kumakh hama yooneloo
Daan naa njulsi njai
Daan naa tuma njulsi njai
Magum njuli duma daan
Billai sipai lippahati koli
Billahati sipahati lippahati koli
Asmali Njai, kai fayli mbaar
Duma fayli mbaar, maa ngai nyibi
Dema tuma Roogoo Roog, Roog Jali Sen
Ma ngai nyibi cha yaa Rasoolu lai
Su nyu janghi, mbaar njai
Su nyu jeegi, mbaar njai
Nyo daan ubi maa daan yorr.

Translated as:

> I waved bye to the *mbaar njai*.
> I did not wave bye again to the *mbaar njai*.
> *Singa joli Maafaal*
> *Tingara tingara loo.*
> Today I pay my dues.
> I have paid it with a whipping cane.
> I no longer pay it with a whipping cane.
> The spiritual protector sent me.
> I was once a newly circumcised;
> But I am no longer newly circumcised.
> The elders of the newly circumcised cannot defeat me.
> I swear to God, *Lippahati Koli.*
> Asmaali Njai, come close the *mbaar.*
> I will not close the mbaar; I am going home.
> I am no longer going to the Serer high god, *Roog Jali Sen.*
> I am returning to the prophet.
> Our girls of the *mbaar njai;*
> Our women of the *mbaar njai,*
> They used to open the doors.
> And I was responsible for the *mbaar.*
> (*Translation by author from oral tradition*)

Some of the *kassaks* are not so elaborate, but they are presented as riddles rich with sexual philosophy that may not be immediately accessible to the layperson and therefore require experienced interpretation. *Kassaks* are notorious for being difficult and cryptic and filled with doctrines of male secrecy. Take, for example, the following:

> *Kopo toli, kopo toli*
> *Tolo li waii*
> *Bo nyi maam dama na*
> *Se meng nyam nyaw na*

Translated as:

Kopo toli, kopo toli
Tolo li waii
Grandpa's teeth have fallen;
But his axe is sharp.
(Translated by author from oral tradition)

The first two lines of the *kassak* are essentially nonsensical sounds, utilized for their music. The mixing of many sounds and languages in a *kassak* is common; it reflects the concern for secret knowledge or wisdom or superstitions, characteristic of the cult of the circumcised. Deliberate attempts to communicate through secret codes rather than directly, gives the *njuli* some newly acquired superior status over the "uncircumcised." The last two lines of the *kassak* refer to the fact that even though "age" may weaken an old man's virility, his sexual prowess finds a revived and rejuvenated expression in the person of his heirs; that is, in his newly circumcised children or grandchildren.

Another *kassak* rich in sexual meaning is one which demonstrates the use of the poem as a "communication code" between the circumcised. The *kassak* goes:

Nja yaanoo, li jaal chi geej
Su ma don toom bal,
Fü la je lee.

Translated as:

O swing, which passes through a river,
If I was to float a boat,
This is where I will fish.
(Translated by author from oral tradition)

This *kassak* is used by a circumcised who meets a girl he loves and wants to communicate it to another circumcised. The "river" here is simply the opportunity for meeting the girl; the "boat" is the vehicle of love (the mechanism for "fishing" for the girl); and the last line of the *kassak* is simply a revelation of choice.

When the period of circumcision is about to end, the initiates are told of a monster (*maam*--which literally translates as "granny") who will come and eat them. D. P. Gamble describes the ritual about *maam*:

> Roaring sounds are heard during the night, and women, girls, and children in the village have to hide indoors. A tall pole with a pot on top, a phallic symbol, but called the toothbrush of *maam*, *soccu maam (or chewing stick of maam)*, is set up mysteriously in the night. Some villages also have a whipping dance in which initiates both give and receive blows with thin rods.[13]

The ritual about *maam* is traditionally accompanied with *kassak*, one of the most popular ones is:

Maamo, maam Sanneh,
Kai jel sa dom ye;

Translated as:

Grandpa, Grandpa Sanneh,
Come take your children.
(Translated by author from oral tradition)

The message of the *kassak* is ritualistic and is intended to instill fear to enable the *njuli* to learn how to conquer it. Adulthood, in essence, requires the mastery of fear.

Overall, Wolof poetic forms reveal a rich ritualistic consistency that depends, to a large extent, on the social context they are utilized in, and the functional requirements of the moment. The poetic forms cannot simply be dismissed as anachronistic, as verbal forms of a bygone era, or as cultural casualties smothered by the menacing wheels of the train of material progress. Instead, the traditional poetic forms have sunk deep root in the Senegambian collective psyche and in existing cultural repertoire. They are, in short, resilient and enduring. Whether be it the *woi* or *taga* or *baaku* or *kassak,* modern adaptations exist which mimic past forms; albeit they are today vulgarized. The *woi*, in particular, has sustained much interest among contemporary practitioners of the Wolof musical arts like Youssou Ndure, Baba Maal, and Ismaila Lo, who no longer just come from the lower castes, but who practice music as a modern profession and who draw from tradition and are today appreciated locally and worldwide in the global musical scene.

Notes

1 David P. Gamble, Linda K. Salmon, and Alhaji Hassan Njie, *Peoples of the Gambia. vol. 1, The Wolof* (San Francisco: D. P. Gamble's Gambian Studies Series, no. 17, 1985), 1.
2 Unknown Senegalese author, "Tradition and Cultural Identity in Senegal (TCIS, unpublished paper, 1991).
3 Ibid.
4 Gamble et al., 16.
5 The concept of *gorr*, apart from suggestions of a person who had traditional rights of self-possession, is also linked to the ability to exercise "use rights" or "ownership claims" on common property. For example, the Wolof refer to *gorr matta* or "claiming ownership of firewood by mixing one's labor with what is given in common, that is, the forest or bush, or simply by cutting down trees."
6 Cheikh Anta Diop, *Precolonial Black Africa* (West Port: Lawrence Hill & Company, 1987), 1.
7 Ibid., 2.
8 Chinua Achebe, *Things Fall Apart* (New York: Fawcett Crest Books, 1969), 7.
9 TCIS, 18.
10 Gamble et al., 28-29.
11 Much of the discussions in this paragraph benefited greatly from my conversations with the late Gambian professor, Dr. Sulayman S. Nyang. He clarified my understanding that *tohal mbaar* was the newly circumcised, so called because he was nearest to the "salivating phase." The youngest among the circumcised is the one, as such, filled most with the 'water of life."
12 A similar poetic form which should be added to the other four poetic forms is *kebe tu* (rap poetry), which is also participatory in nature and relies on a call-response and exploitation of syncopated rhythms. It combines rhythmic repetition, street philosophy with folk vulgarity, and is often humorous. A popular Senegambian *kebetu* is *Bai Cham, kai jai ma guru*, or Bai Cham, come and sell me kolanuts.
13 Ibid., 29.

CHAPTER 3

TOWARD A WOLOF METAPHYSICS AND PHILOSOPHY: SOME PRELIMINARY REFLECTIONS

Wolof Concept of the Human (Nit)

The Wolof of Senegal and The Gambia (Senegambia) are an articulate people for whom speech is a daily staple in which they engage in selectively, using sound, symbol, and sign. The Wolof value speech so much that they say, *Wakh moi nit* or "Speech is the person." Conversations--- or the interactive process of people sharing meaning between themselves by choosing their words carefully (*wakhtaan*)--are an enjoyable pastime, an interactive process where the speaker throws his voice (*sani baat*) and the partner in the dialogue listens, weighs the content, and calibrates a response.

Wolof value humans (*nit*). But the value and validation of a *nit* is in other *nits*. *Nit nitai garabam*, the Wolof say—implying, "A person is the medicine of another person." The cliché, "no person is an island" unto themselves borrowed from John Donne, is alive and well among the Wolof. A person exists in a society in which they are born, in which they will work, invent, pursue leisure, procreate, raise children, collaborate with family, friends and neighbors, and finally die. The person must respect themselves, what the Wolof called *fonka bopa*. Respecting oneself is conducting oneself in ways that meet societal approval. However, respecting oneself is not to be bloated with pride (*beewu*) or to be engaged in fanfaronade. *Beewu*, or "foolish pride," is an act of vanity and self-infatuation; whereas *fonka bopa* is an act of self-dignity.

The Wolof never elevate a human to the status of God. *Nit nit rek la* or "Humans are only humans," and *Yaala Yaala la* or *Yaala Yaana* or "God is God," and "God is the infinite." This is the ontological tautology. The attempt to elevate a human to the level of God comes from human arrogance. It is human's attempt to put a "halo" on another mere, undeserving human. Humans can never be God. The Wolof say, *Ludut yala neen la* that "Whatever is not God must be ordinary." This is part of the leveling philosophy of the Wolof. One may respect humans for their intelligence, beauty, physical strength, wealth, and moral uprightness, but one should never elevate them to the status of God. Humans may have extraordinary qualities, but they eventually succumb to the rudimentary laws of nature— *dundah* and *deey* or "birth" and "death." In fact, the Wolof say, *Luy dundah fok mu deey*, or "Whatever lives must die," whereas God never dies.

The human person comprises several components: *yaram* (physical body), *yurr* or *hel* (brain, mind), *fit* (courage), and *sagoe* (self-regulating spirit, that which balances the self, self-consciousness). The biological components of the "human body" or *yaram* are--*yurr* (brains) and *yagh* (bones), *derr* (skin) and *sedet* (muscle), *yapah* (flesh), and *deret* (blood). Proper balance between these physical and psychological components of the self is necessary for a balanced human.

The *nit* is subject to the demands of duality in biological functions:

- *eewu* (waking) versus *nelaaw* (sleeping);
- *leka* (eating) versus *poop* (defecation);
- *naan* (drink) versus *seben* (urination) and *nyahaa* (sweat);
- *hahataai* (uproarious laughter) versus *merr* (anger);
- *nuka* or *lal* (sex) versus *baayi* (abstinence);
- *nop* (erotic love) versus *tongoo* (malice);
- *reeh* (laughing) versus *joi* (crying);
- *dogh* (walking) or *daaw* (running) versus *noopalu* (resting), and

- *chiipu* (mouth teasing), or *wolis* (whistling, ululation) versus *noopi* (silence, quietness).

Nit is also subject to a social scale, honed on the asperity of the times. The Wolof speak of *nit bu am soloh* (a person of consequence) or *nit bu amul soloh* (a person without consequence). The person with *soloh* has to be taken seriously because, for them, they mean their words-- they act on their words. A person with *soloh* is one of responsibility and accountability. A person "without *soloh*," conversely, cannot be taken seriously. Words to them are just pliant gimmickry, used for *hajaan* (to boast) or *poh/foh* (to play), but there is little consequence to their words. The Wolof word, *soloh*, is easily utilized as a metaphysical scale of value to accommodate or to dismiss a person or event as having consequence or as lacking in consequence (i.e., *nyaakah soloh*).

In the traditional Wolof universe, humans (*nit*) follow a unidirectional trajectory of birth (*judu*), death (*dey*) to rebirth (y*aadikone*), where one dies and returns to earth. Wolof, in short, believe in a form of reincarnation in life following a unilinear path of cyclicality. The following diagram on human life illustrates that. The Wolof have a saying that *Pitaakh luumu naaw naaw, fok mu taak,* or "No matter how much a pigeon flies, it must come to rest." Death is the ultimate first rest—and the transition zone to *yadikone* (rebirth). When a person is born, they have an infinite possibility of options that a life can take. However, there are some fixed parameters to which is added an overlay of custom and tradition, which complicates or enriches a person's life. A person is born into the caste of the nobility (*gerr*) or of the lower caste (*nyenyo*). The lower castes (*nyenyo*) were divided into various artisanal trades: metal workers (*tega*), musicians (*gewel*), and leather workers (*ude*). Being born into a lower caste, however, did not translate into lower economic opportunity; it simply meant that one had to give social precedence to the nobility (even if the member of the nobility is poorer). A person born into nobility could not marry into the lower castes. The gate between castes was socially guarded in a strict fashion. Often, however, there were trespassers. If a person of a noble caste interloped with one of a low caste, the child from the marriage would be called *sani*, or literally, a child "thrown away." This rigid adherence to caste used to be firm in the old days. Caste prejudice used to be prevalent in The Gambia and in Senegal up to the 1970s, but it is increasingly disappearing, and for good reasons. The caste system is a manifestation of received social rigidity and intolerance. My friend, the late professor Sulayman S. Nyang, recounted to me the story of a girl of low caste in The Gambia of the 1950s, who, as was the custom between admiring lovers, once sewed a handkerchief for a boyfriend from the nobility to express her love. The mother of the boy, upon learning of this, thought this benign act to be so reprehensible that she proceeded to bathe her son with ashes from burned firewood to remove the "caste pollution" which had befallen her son. Such an extreme act of "purification" from "caste pollution" would be considered crazy in these days of enlightenment and caste fluidity, but such was the caste prejudice that existed in the olden days. Today, the caste system is being slowly abolished, and for good reasons. There is growing recognition that a person born into a lower caste should not be condemned forever in that status simply because of the misfortune of birth. The colonial order helped accelerate and put a death nail on the coffin of caste: it helped give members of the lower caste Western education, which in turn conferred economic and social privilege on them over those of the nobility. Today, there are many persons from lower castes in The Gambia and in Senegal, who are occupying relatively higher economic and other privileged positions. Modernity is creating more and more of a society based on merit rather than on heredity, and this is a good thing. The Wolof have a saying, *Sunu, suma ko gen* or "This is ours; this is mine is better." What you can do for yourself is comparatively better than what society hereditarily ascribes to you.

Dundu Nit (Human Life) According to the Wolof: A Diagram

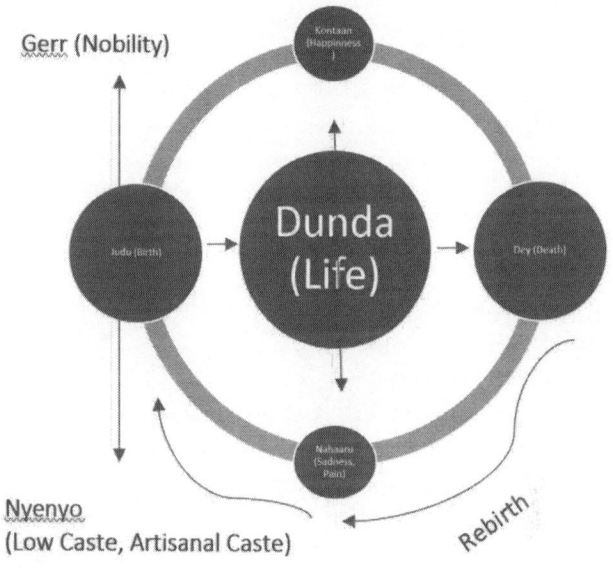

(Diagram developed by author)

When a child is born among the Wolof, when the human is a baby at its most helpless stage, the baby is called *lirr*. When the child reaches the stage of the toddler, the child is referred to as *nguneh*. The toddler would have then passed the state of crawling (*raam*) to standing (*tahaaw*) and beginning to walk (*dogh*). To fortify the steps as the child walked, Wolof adults superstitiously would often follow the infirm walks of the child with a pestle, giving a light pound to the ground against every step a child makes and leaves behind. When a child matures into a teenager and reaches puberty, the Wolof refer to boys as *wahambaanneh* and girls as *jankha*. A mother would proudly refer to his teenage boy as *Mom kaing wahambaanneh la* or "He is now a grown-up teenager with the capacity to impregnate and to produce an offspring." When a child reaches adulthood, the child is referred to as a *makk*.

Wolof Concept of Time

What is time? The Wolof refer to time as *lu tega* or literally, as what beats (Some use the term *wahtu* for time, but that is from the Arabic influence). The markers of time are associated with the "drumbeat," which signals particular events or moments that govern the lives of Wolof people. When a Wolof person meets another, they ask the question, *Nyaataa tega?* which literarily translates as, "How much beats?" -- a clear reference to the signaling effects of the drum of a town crier alerting people to a specific time.

The Wolof conception of "time" is like a "landscape" -- a linear unfolding that stretches back into the "birthplace of time" and extends into the infinite "graveyard of time" —in short we could talk of a "timescape" extending from initial infinity to aspirational infinity. Neat distinctions are drawn by the Wolof between *daymba* or "yesterday," *teye* or "today" and *alek* or "tomorrow," in short between "past," "present," and "future." The past, however, is not forgotten; it continues to have an active presence and influence in the lives of today. People visit graveyards of their ancestors; sing about the great deeds of people of the past; and revere shrines and relics of great peoples of the past.

The Wolof view of time has a "micro" and "macro" dimension. When one looks at "microtime" -- for example, *bes bi* or "the day"-- it is broken into *suba* or morning, *takusaan* or afternoon, *ngonn* or evening, and *guddi* or night. The neat distinctions of the different slices of the day is heliocentric: morning as when daylight emerges; afternoon as when the sun is at its zenith, evening as when the sun fades but there is still light, and night as when the sun disappears and goes to sleep, and darkness rules. Within the "morning," the Wolof make distinctions between "early morning" or *suba tell*, and "late morning" or *suba bu mujay*. In the afternoon, the Wolof make a distinction about a period of intense heat when people generally take shelter and rest and various spirits are believed to creep in or *yorr yorr*. At night, the Wolof also make a distinction about the "onset of night" or *timis* and *haaji gudi* or literarily "halfway into the night" or "midnight." Wolof superstition has it that the onset of the night or *timis* is a time to avoid walking in the streets alone, especially under large trees, because various evil spirits are most active, and it is a time to take refuge and to be home.

The Wolof also have a "macro" conception of time--- which is lunar-centric. The Wolof refer to the month as *fan werr* or as the "days of the moon." Often, they will just refer to the "month" as *werr* or as "the moon." The beginning of the month is referred to as *werr bu dorreh* or "when the moon begins" and the "end of the month" is referred to as *werr bu deiyeh* or when "the moon dies." The lunar cycle, of course, follows a full moon, a half moon, a quarter moon, to a disappeared moon or literarily the "moon dying." The moon, however, goes through continuous rebirths and deaths to make the lunar calendar. Twelve moons make up one year or *att*. It is unclear whether this twelve-month system is based on Western Euro-Chrisitian or on Arabo-Islamic influences or was always there among the Wolof. Usually, concepts introduced into the Wolof universe will maintain a foreign reference. The Wolof, however, have an indigenous name for years-- *att*, suggesting that it is an indigenous concept. How many moons make up an *att*--- however--- could have been influenced by external forces.

Another dimension in the Wolof's conception of "macro-time" is the concept of *jamano* or "generation." *Jamano* refers to large chunks of time over which people make grand history. Njaga Mbye, the famous Senegalese *khalam* (banjo) folk singer of the 1970s, used to say, *Jamano kuko fekeeh war saa def lu baakh; jamanoo, lu wey sa ganaaw laa*, or "A generation, whoever witnesses it should do good in it; for a generation transpires after you, captures your individual record." A generation, of course, allows a large swathe of time to pass through which people can make history, move through time's chasm to redeem themselves as heroes or as villains.

Apart from concepts associated with the metaphysics of time, there is a utilitarian use of time in the Wolof universe. Because the Wolof are traditionally an agrarian people, the use of time was often linked to the agricultural calendar. Central to this use of time was the "rainy season" or *nawet* when the "rains" or *taw* are expected almost daily between late July to November. When the rain clouds gather, the Wolof refer to that period as *kheen*. When it drizzles with sunlight---the Wolof refer to that as the "hyena's rain" or as the *tawi bukki*. Often the *Bawu naan* or "rain dance" would be engaged in to appeal to the heavens or to the "gods" to bring rain. Then there is the period of clearing and preparing the land, often into furrows that can capture water and fix it into the root zones of the plants--- this is the period known as *tangi beye*. The *beye kat* or "farmer," after seeding their crop, does periodic weeding and tending until the "harvest period" or the *beyi toll*. Much of the cereals grown in Wolof farms are millet and coos (*duguub*), cassava (*nyaambi*), maize (*mbooha*), peanuts (*gerteh*), and beans (*nyebeh*). Wolof women grow the vegetables (such as, lettuce, peppers, okra, assorted folk greens, tomatoes, onions, carrots, and cabbages.).

The Wolof conception of time is not precise--- time is not measured by the second or by the minute or by the hour, but by approximation to the motions of the sun in a day. The Wolof, like most cultures, divide the day between work and leisure. Early morning is for hard work, midday for siesta because it is when the sun is hottest, and late afternoon to early evening is for work resumption, followed by rest in late evening and night. The afternoon "siesta" or *nopal* or "rest" is often carried out under the shade of a "tree" or *kerr* --and usually there are logs, wooden benches, or chairs for seating and conversing or *wakhtaan*. Elders often distinguish themselves by resting on a reclining seat or rocking chair called *pliyaan*.

In Western society, reference is often made to the "time value of money" or *Halisi teye nekul halisi alek* or "A money unit today is not the same as a money unit tomorrow." This is essentially to capture inflation and interest. In Wolof society, until the advent of Islam and Christianity, these were alien concepts. If a person borrowed a certain sum of money, he repaid it by the same amount later, regardless of the fact that the value of that same sum may have been eroded by inflation, or it deprived the lender of the possible use of the funds while it was being lent out. Similarly, when it comes to the "money value of time," the Wolof seem to place less value to time outside of the period of work. This may simply be an orientation based on agrarian values, where, outside of farming work, people seem to put a premium on enjoying each other's company rather than attaching pecuniary value to time.

Conception of time also varies according to the status of individuals in society. When an important person (*borom dolleh* or *borom marhama*) calls, one should hasten to respond to the call. However, upon arrival, it is not uncommon to wait for that important person until they are ready to attend to one. The reverse holds true for an unimportant person (*ku amul soloh*—"one without consequence" or *ku nyaka kaatan*—"one who is poor or weak"). Why does status matter in the "valuing of time" differently among the Wolof? It is the age-old question of how even the use of time is altered by the distribution and asymetries of power and status in society.

Wolof Concept of Space

The Wolof refer to space as *yaatu kai* or literally "the clearing where something can dwell." Some use the term *diggante* or literally "between objects" or *jawwu* to refer to space. Space has meaning only because of some fixed references, some fixed points. The delimitations of space is often relative, in relation to a natural object: a tree (*garab*), a mountain (*tunda*) or stone/rock (*herr*), a stream (*gej*), or a heavenly body or an artificial object (*ligaye yu nit*). More broadly, the Wolof refer to "space on earth" as *yaatu kayi suff* or "the waters" as *yaatu kayi gej* or the "sky" or "heavens" as *yaatu kayi asaaman*.

When one looks at space on the earth, for example, town planning (*jaagalu deku waaye*), the various uses of space figure prominently. In the use of space, the Wolof emphasize social cohesion and communal stability, safety, hygiene, functionality, and beauty. For large villages or settlements (*deku waaye*) or (*pencha*), the Wolof emphasize social cohesion by dividing them into functional quarters (*gogh-bi*). For example, the Wolof may allow people to settle together in a given quarter because they are newcomers to the village and therefore have special needs that could be better served by concentration. While I was growing up in The Gambia, in the town of Serrekunda, we had an entire quarter of settlements by the *fana fana* or rural Wolofs from up-country. In fact, the street came to be known as *Fana street*.

When we consider space in the waters, there is much that is unknown and much that is a mystery. The technology of sea exploration among the Wolof was limited to canoes and boats and human diving skills. The Wolof fished the waters and occasionally would encounter a creature or object never seen or thought of before. The Wolof often say, *Ndoghi gej, lu doi waar la* or the "Sea waters are filled with awe." In the waters are fish (*jen*), turtles (*mbonat*), snails (*yet*), oysters (*yokhos*), shrimps (*poho poho*), crocodiles (*jasiit*), and several indescribable and undiscovered creatures and plants.

Concerning space in the heavens, there are the heavenly bodies known to the Wolof: moon (*werr bi*), sun (*janta bi*), *bidiw yi* (the stars), and clouds (*nirr*). The heavens, like the sea, is characterized by unfathomable forces and mysteries. Through the space of the heavens, we have forces of evaporation and rain (*taw*); thunder (*dennu, haadar*) and lightning (*melehi asamaan*); storms/winds (*ngelaw*) and scorching heat (*natchwu tanga*). The sky is the domain of the theater of countless flying creatures, from birds (*picha yi*) to bats (*njugub* yi) to bees (*yomba-yi*) to flies (*weing-yi*).

In the utilization of space on earth, the Wolof focus on community needs and on hygiene. In a typical Wolof village, the entire village is usually protected by a fence (*saaket*) to ward off wild animals and hostile strangers (*gan yu bon*). On the outskirts of the perimeters of the village would be the village farms (*tolls*); they also would be protected with fences. Individual households may opt for their own private fences to protect their individual property and also to dig their own family wells (*tayn*) and family latrines (*kama*). Considerable effort is put to separate, with reasonable distance, the location of the wells from the pit latrines to avoid groundwater pollution. This is part of the hygiene-emphasis of the Wolof in village planning. Structures such as the kitchen (*wayng*) and stores/barns (*pukus*) are also located in the family compound, taking into account hygiene and convenience.

Wolof Concept of Numbers

Numbers are crucial to the Wolof's ability to rationalize their environment. The Wolof use both cardinal and ordinal numbers to describe their universe. Cardinal numbers are utilized in counting and in defining quantitative magnitudes. In counting, the Wolof have a base-ten counting system with subbase five. This perhaps might come from the fact that the Wolof use their hands to count, and one has five fingers in one hand and ten fingers when one combines the right and left hands. The Wolof system of counting is as follows:

Wolof Number	English Equivalent
Bena	One
Nyarr	Two
Nyetta	Three
Nyenent	Four
Juroom	Five
Juroom Bena	Five plus One (= Six) – Subbase Five
Juroom Nyarr	Five plus Two (=Seven)
Juroom Nyetta	Five plus Three (=Eight)
Juroom Nyenent	Five plus Four (=Nine)
Fuka	Ten -------------------------Base Ten

Once one counts to ten (*fuka*), the Wolof repeat the *Fuka ak Bena* (Ten plus One) and the series goes to a subbase five, and then rises up to base ten. The base ten numbers are:

Fuka	Ten
Nyarr Fuka	Two Tens (= Twenty)
Nyetta Fuka	Three Tens (=Thirty)
Nyenent Fuka	Four Tens (=Fourty)
Juroom Fuka	Five Tens (=Fifty)
Juroom Bena Fuka	Six Tens (=Sixty)

Juroom Nyarr Fuka	Seven Tens (=Seventy)
Juroom Nyetta Fuka	Eight Tens (=Eighty)
Juroom Nyenent Fuka	Nine Tens (=Ninety)
Temmerr	One Hundred
Junneh	One Thousand
Alfung/Junniy junneh	Million

Because traditionally, Wolof societies were small and largely agrarian, counting was influenced by the use of small numbers. One rarely encountered numbers in the billions or trillions. As such, the use of infinitely large numbers in today's Wolof lexicon simply borrows from the Western languages. Large numbers are basically the invention of agglomeration economies in cities, where everything is amplified to a giant scale. The advent of the city can largely be argued as the product of advancement with the development of public infrastructure and markets for goods and services. It was suddenly discovered that, by people crowding together in a contiguous space, they can reduce the cost of the delivery of shared or network goods and services like roads, potable water, and electricity to themselves.

The Wolof use of a number, such as *bena* or "one," is an archetypal abstraction. It refers to an abstract singularity that is adjectival. It precedes the description of the object to tell us how many of the object there is, such as *bena garab* or "one tree," or *nyarr garab* or "two trees." When one talks about *bena*, one speaks of a "generic one" from which all "specific ones" flow. (Some may dispute that this is the way in which the Wolof think; that one is imposing Platonic logic to Wolof metaphysics.) But the agrarian environment the Wolof traditionally operated under combines the world of generalization and abstraction, as manifested in concepts of spirits and supernatural beings, as well as of particularity.

The Wolof use ordinal numbers to designate rank, order, or position. They add "*el*" to the cardinal numbers to designate *ordinality*, as follows:

Number	English Equivalent
Njekel	First
Nyaarel	Second
Nyetel	Third
Nyenetel	Fourth
Juroombel	Fifth
Juroombenel	Sixth

It is important to note that "first" is not referred to as *benel* deriving from the Wolof one *bena* but as *njekel* or "what precedes everything" or "what precedes all numbers."

The Wolof also use numbers to draw functional relationships. For example, the Wolof use the term *yookal* or *doolli* to refer to "addition." Addition is incremental, making a "figure" bigger by joining a quantity to it. Because the Wolof use a lot of ordinary chemistry in cleaning, cooking, building, metal working, and so on, the concept of "addition" is very important in pursuing daily functional life. Similarly, "subtraction" or *waanyi* is an important functional relationship. Another term used for "subtraction" is *gayneh* or literarily "to take out." In trading relationships in the market, the Wolof would bargain for a lower price for a good--- they will use directly, *Manneh waanyil ma tuuti*, or "Please, reduce the cost a little." With the seller wanting to add to the price and the buyer wanting to subtract, the market works at the margin, until a satisfactory price is agreed on. Usually, depending on the desperation of the seller, the seller yields to nearer a reservation price, by reducing the price and by squeezing their profit-margin to make a sale. After a sale, the buyer says, *Jere jeff* or "Thank you" and may shake hands with the seller in appreciation.

The Wolof also use *haajale* or *seedale* or "division" to share goods among a population of beneficiaries. In a household, parents always perform the delicate act of the "division" of household goodies among members, especially children, all the time. In business, in a joint enterprise, the parties also perform a division of revenues. The functional role of "division" is a priori straightforward; however, when applied unequally in the social distribution of goods and services, it can have ethical dimensions of fairness or unfairness. In fact, children in Wolof households, especially stepchildren or adopted children who are treated unfairly, automatically understand experientially the concept of unfair division. Because they often get shortchanged in the social division of household goodies, this often creates feelings of "envy" or "jealousy" or *anyaan* among them. The Wolof often say, *Doomi jütlee du doom* or "A stepchild is not a child," referring to the "envy" that shapes their character.

The Wolof concept of multiplication may appear less precise. The Wolof refer to "multiples" as *lu barri* or simply as "plenty" and "multiply" as *barril* or "to make plenty." However, multiplication can be understood as a complex operation of addition—and in that sense it is precise. It is understandable that a fertile and well-watered farm will yield plenty of grain or multiple of grain; however, the precise nature of these multiples eventually will require measuring them in a calabash or in some local grain container. If one asks a traditional Wolof farmer with a productive farm, how much multiples of sorghum that planting one gunny sack of sorghum would yield, he would say, *lu barri* or "plenty." Alternatively, the farmer may resort to a more precise measurement through the use of traditional containers of measurement, such as calabashes or gourds. In a sense, perhaps, multiplication is a function popular when dealing with complex settings and large numbers. In the traditional agrarian life of the Wolof, routine mathematical transactions often required addition, subtraction, and division and rarely multiplication. However, multiplication, after all is, is only a shortcut for addition.

The Wolof also use the concept of equations and inequalities to describe and to comprehend their physical and relational universe. For example, the concept of an equation is not unfamiliar when dealing with measuring weight, such as grain, on a balance. The Wolof use the word *pesse* to refer to weighing, putting objects on a balance, on a scale, to determine if their weights are equal. They also use inanimate and animate objects to draw comparisons. For example, a large person may be compared to an elephant or *koku da fa raye ni nyai* or, if small, compared to a mouse, *koku da fa tutti ni janakh*.

Wolof Proverbs

Ku yarru, fallu: The person who is disciplined or well-mannered ultimately rules. (Playing by the rules ultimately pays.)

Raw ma jikkoh, ma dabelaa lamenge: Surpass me with good works and I will surpass you with my tongue. (Good people can be undermined by spin doctors.)

Rewe lamenge, gaata gaanaye: A person with an insolent tongue is always short on weaponry. (Foul speech lands one into trouble. Guard one's tongue or be prepared for negative consequences.)

Lamenge, paaka nyaari boorla: The tongue is a two-sided knife. (It can cut both ways; so guard it with reason.)

Ku noopam werr, du raagal wakh hi ku febarr: A healthy ear can withstand the fever of sick words. (A good listener can deciper and moderate even the ugliest of messages.)

Lu neg fes fes, jar gong def fa neg gam: No matter how full the house, a spider always finds space for a nest.

Ndogh mu tuuru moo gen ndaal mu toch: Spilling water is better than breaking the jar.

Fokatal, daanu, waarul nga bayi dow bi: Falling while running does not mean you should give up the race.

Ku def sukur si buteil bu ubbi warrul ragaal melentaan: A person who keeps sugar in an open jar should not fear the visit of ants.

Su ngelaw barree si gech, kena neh neng deelu, kenen ne neng continee, hamgen ne huloo dorr na: When storms gather at sea, one sailor says let us go and another says no; know a quarrel is about to start.

Su picha yaageh si garaab, haleeyi jam ko: When a bird stays too long on a tree, it will receive the wrath of stone throwers.

Lu gech fes, fes, man na jeel ndogh: However full a river is, it will not refuse to take in more water.

Kakatarr bu sol sa yeereh beteye kakatarr la: A chameleon pretending to wear the colors of your clothes is still a chameleon.

Kuy nobu chi roni garaab munuul feheh taw bum ko lal: Someone hiding under a tree cannot prevent raindrops from touching them.

Haaleh yaa ngiy joy, maak nyi teetal leen: Kids coil in woe when elders frighten them with lies.

Ku duga chi gaali nyu deger bopa, alek mu raychu: Joining the boat of the stubborn-headed often leads to the shores of regret.

Fu muus ak jaanakh fanaan chi jaama, tawmi mo takh: When a cat shares shelter with a mouse, it is because of the rain.

Fu nit yi nangoo fenkat, dega dee: When people get used to falsehoods, then even truth loses its luster.

Jen bu judoo chi ndogh, magee chi ndogh, warrul raggal ndogh: A fish born in water, that grew in water, cannot fear water.

Jikko ak borom mam nyo anda: Character and its owner go together until the grave.

Nyaha du feign chi taw: Sweat is invisible in the rain.

Sani dara chi biti tahul janta bi jok: A thing put out to dry cannot cause the sun to rise.

Ganarr du yoneeh bukki chi domam: A wise hen does not send a hyena as an emissary to her chicks.

So reree, tahawaal nyaanal jamaa sa bopa: Any time you lose your way, pick yourself up and throw yourself a good wish.

Moto du dawaal bopaam: A car does not run itself alone.

Ku naatu baari mboka; ku nyaaka du am mboka: Success grows your relatives and failure repels them.

Ku lakaa mburu sampa raywe: A person who bakes bread builds a country.

Ku taal safaara, worr ko feey: A person who lights a bushfire should fetch water to put it out.

Maata na, du maata, li gen buul dugaal sa loho chi gaymeng nyam: Whether a creature bites or does not bite matters, but the safest thing is not to put your hand in its mouth.

Maak du haalel: An adult is not a child.

Ku tufli chi asamaan, harkanaam toy: The person who spits at the sky only gets their face wet.

Dega, kaani la: Truth is like hot pepper; it burns where lies proliferate.

Kuy deeh, weehu: A person faced with the specter of death must shake.

Ku rerr sa kanaam opaa la pehee: If a person you need escapes in front of your face, they must be superior in tricks.

So eggul chi geeni yoon, contineel di dokh: So long as you have not come to the end of the road, keep walking.

Ku musuul neekka taalibe, munnul nek sering daara: One who has never been a student cannot be be a good teacher.

Burr aayul, dag yi nyo aay: A king is not evil; it is the courtiers who are.

Ku munaalut bopaam daara, manul sopee aduna: A persona unable to take care of themselves cannot be an agent of transformation for the world.

Mbota bugga na ndogh, waayy buggul ndogh mu taanga: A toad likes water, but not hot water.

Bugal dunda teeh dundal bu baakh: Love life to live it well and live life to love it well.

Jikko mo gen taarr: Character or good manners are better than beauty.

Picha man na naaw chi kow wandeh heelam munkh chi suuf: A bird may fly high, but it always has its mind on grain on the ground.

Haaleh bu yaaru, fallu: A child well trained is one step ahead on the road to prosperity.

Ku muun, muun: A person who is patient smiles in the end.

Bala ngaa utti jabarr walla jekkar, uttil goro: Before you seek a wife or husband, look for good in-laws.

Nyaye du nobu chi ronni lal: An elephant will not hide under a bed.

Ndanka, ndanka, jaappa golo: By moving slowly, slowly, one can catch a monkey.

Nit, nitai garaabam: The best medicine for a person is another person.

Geeni golo guda na, waaye lu ko laal mu yekk ko: No matter how long a monkey's tail is, if you touch it, it will know.

Jaambar neekul dogh chi yoon ba jaan bi demee: Bravery is not trampling the path of a snake after it is gone.

Ludut yaala neen la: Whatever is not God must be ordinary.

So noba ham ham chi nyi jaangul, dugal ko chi terree: If you want to hide knowledge from an illiterate, put it in a book.

Saama-kat nyaari ett la aam, botaam ak eetam: A shepherd has two weapons, his eyes and his staff/stick.

Banta lumu yaaga yaaga chi gej, du suppaleku jaasit: No matter how long a log is in a river, it will not turn into a crocodile.

Mbaam du jurr si kanaami nit: A donkey does not give birth in front of people.

Ludut yaala du burr: Whatever is not God cannot be king.

Ku haamul dek yi neeka chi yooni daymba, bes bu nekka, dek matta ko: People who do not understand the thorns of the past get pricked every day.

Goudi moodi burri kerr: Night is the king of shades.

Ku bot bukki, khaj bow la: If you keep the company of hyenas, dogs will bark at you.

Golo nyaawul, bayaam la nyuru: A monkey is not ugly; it resembles its father.

Ku yaala meei, mu am: To whom God gives, they must have.

Lu fenn bari, bari, su dega jogay, jot ko: No matter how lies proliferate, if truth rises it will catch up with it.

Burr bu amul nit du burr: A subjectless king is not a king.

Banta bu yaala taal, ken munu ko fei: The firewood that God had lit, no human can extinguish.

Jaapal sa harit ak nyaari lohoh; sa noon ak nyaari bot: Hold a friend with two hands and an enemy with two eyes.

Ku parree wut borree aduna, aduna dana borri passe ko: If you are not prepared to wrestle with the world, the world will wrestle to meet you.

Lu pitakh now, now; fok mu takk: No matter how much the pigeon flies, it has to land.

Ganaar degaat na doom mam, waye bang nu ko: A fowl steps on its chick, but does not dislike it.

Ndimbal war na fekkeeh lohoh borom mam: Helping a needy person requires their own hands already on deck.

Jambarr chi jeff ju baakh du waanyi nit: Courage in doing good does not diminish a person.

Lu khale tahau gisu ko, mak tog gis ko: What a child standing does not see, an elder can sit and see.

Ki gen chi nit yi moi nyi dimbaale nit yi; ki bon moi kiy gaing nit yi: The best among us are those who benevolently help others; the worse are those who maliciously harm others.

Baing, jaan la bu noy yaaram, wai dangaarr ram man na rei nit: Hate is a snake whose body is soft, but its venom is deadly.

Boppa bu am njering, noppa munk si saakh: A head that is useful, that is together, is well coordinated with its ears.

Won ma sa kharit, ma wakh la sa jikko: Show me your friend, and I will tell you your character.

So feekkeh nyuy huloo, wohal degga: If you witness parties to a dispute, always speak the truth.

Makyaa nekul bejaaw rek: Gray hair alone does not make an elder.

Bugail so ko nobeeh daf lai gaing: Love when hidden can wound you.

Gan du ewwi beyy: A stranger or visitor does not untie the goats of their host.

Burr du mbokka: A king is not a relative.

Finga dorreh du sa mujjeh: Your beginning is not your destiny.

Buga sa dom kom haalis la, wai sa dom bugala lolu urus la: Loving your children is silver, but your children loving you back is more precious than gold.

Nyaaka ham baakhul wai ku nanguta jaanga moo gena bon: Ignorance is bad, but refusing to learn is worse.

Sei harrela: Marriage is war with the weapons of love.

Ku waakh waakhul, ki jootali mo waakh: The person who spoke has not spoken; it is the transmitter of tales who spoke.

Lu khalee waakh chi biti, chi kerram la ko jangee: What a child says outside, they learn from home.

Soo dul sol mbahanah bu am dej, bul ko jokh nyenen nyi nyu sol: If the hat you try to wear has thorns that hurt your head, please do not give it to others to wear.

Suuf bu kheef moi def nit yu kheef: Hungry soils lead to hungry people.

Coka bui tomba chi digi gech faalewul ndoghi taw: A cork floating at the extreme depths of the sea is not afraid of rainwater.

Nyaari kui du nyu boka mbalka: Two lead bulls do not share the same wooden watering trough.

Ku laal geenu gaindeh, laal na lukoi torohal: If you finger the tail of lion, you are asking for trouble.

Wolof Values

I have noted in my book for young adults, *Wolof*,[1] that the Wolof see the person or *nit* as operating in a social universe, and the Wolof put great emphasis on social belonging. In fact, as mentioned earlier, they have a saying, *Nit nitai garabam* (A person is the medicine of another person). A person lives in a society, but one's social well-being is linked to respecting and following community values. Perhaps the two most important values are *jom* (dignity, or self-respect) and *ham-sa-bop* (self-knowledge). The Wolof also value *ham-ham* (wisdom, knowledge); *bakh* (goodness, kindness), *terranga* (hospitality), *dega* (honesty), *set* (cleanliness), *moun* (patience), *tegin* (good manners), *kersa* (respect for others), and *yarru* (discipline). A person's social rating is often linked to how well they respect these values.

There are also other Wolof values such as appreciation of the beautiful. The Wolof use the term *raafet* (used to refer to external beauty for subjects and objects) and *taar* (used to refer only to beauty in humans, specifically women--- including their inner beauty).

A person must also respect the environment. The Wolof draw important lessons from nature. Largely an agricultural people, they recognize the importance of natural elements such as the land, water, air, and fire in safeguarding their existence. The Wolof even have a saying that *Ku yaaha dekkam, yaahana luko jeering* or *Ku yaaha dendam, yaahana luko jeering* or "A person who mistreats nature mistreats what benefits him." The code word for right living is balance.

Wolof Philosophers

The Wolof have many philosophers, but their thoughts, because of the absence of the documentary record since all thought is conveyed by word of mouth, have disappeared into the grayeyard of oral tradition. Because oral tradition is based on the culture of consensus, heretical ideas get weeded out by the rule of natural selection and some go extinct. One philosopher, from the sixteenth century, who stands out, and it is not clear why, is Kochy Barma Faal. Kochy was close to the king of Cayor (the Damel of Cayor), Damel Daaw Demba Faal, and perhaps that closeness to power may have earned him distinction for his sayings and for his philosophical discourses. Some of his wise statements appear as direct observations of operations in the court of the king.

Kochy was born with the name Birima Makhureja Demba Khole Faal and lived from 1586 (some put it from 1584) to 1655 (some put it from 1654) or thereabouts. He was a member of the Serer *laman* (master of the land; noble) caste. He was born in the village of Njonge Faal in the area of Ndande, Louga, in present day Senegal. One might wonder how could a Serer be a Wolof philosopher, but the interchange between Wolof and Serer cultures has been one of intermarriages and unified syncretism throughout the ages.

One of the descendants of Kochy, Alhajji Ndongo Faal, gives us some insights about his distinguished ancestor. He notes that Kochy was a thinker, a teacher, an adviser to the king, an arbiter of disputes, and a social therapist. In his discourses, Kochy operated in a question and answer mode. For example, when Kochy was asked: what does a person do who wants to have peace in this world and peace in the afterlife? He responded that a person who wants peace in this world must abide by the dictates of the king. If a person wants peace in the afterlife, one needed to follow the dictates of the King of the Afterlife, the Owner of the Afterlife. This shows that Kochy had a pragmatic understanding of the relation between peace and power. In whatever domain a person operated in, if one wanted peace, one had to follow the rules of the dominant power in that domain.

A second question that Kochy was asked was what did he know about the relation between *maagny*i (elders) and *guuneh yi* (children). He notes that children should respect elders, but that elders should protect and have pity (*yerem*) for children. He notes that *guuneh* (children) and *ndow* (youths) are not the same. He notes that children should be guided (*digal*), helped/supported (*dimbali*), and protected (*saama*). Youths (*ndow*), however, are different from children and childhood because they are entering early maturity. They have a capability (*nyu am dooleh*) to take care of themselves and for thoughtful independent action. They are the assets of the future (*yaakari alek*). He notes that *Ndow denyu maaga te maagetenwunyul*, meaning, "Youths are close to maturity but not yet old."

A third question that Kochy was asked is how does one operate within one's times (*dohaali jamano*). He answered that when one exists in one's time, one must handle matters according to how urgent they are. There is the immediate-(*jamano tell*), the medium-term (*seelu jamano*), and the long-term future (*jublu bu eleg*). There is also the issue on what weight to put on persons and what weight to put on words. Kochy argued that a person's life is finite (*nit guduul fan*) but that words are infinitely lived (*wakh da fa gudu faan*). Because words are infinitely lived, they have to be shepherded and used carefully.

A fourth question that he was asked is how do people handle their relations, and how do villages handle their difficulties (*jaafe jaafe*). He was an acute social observer. For humans, he observed that the four critical components in human relations are *jom* (dignity, self-respect); *fuula* (self-discipline); *faida* (mindfulness), and *ngorr* (nobility). Kochy also observed human imperfections. Humans, he noted, have the following tendencies. They love and hate (*de nyu baaga di baanj*). They gain/acquire and lose (*de nyu am di nyaaka*). They get well and are sick (*de nyu werr di werradi*). They practice openness and closeness, depending on the circumstance (*de nyu ubi di tej*). In terms of settling difficulties in a village, Kochy argued there are those who would require a big stick (*lu faj dorr*), those who require conversations (*lu faj wakh*), and those who require patience (*lu faj muing*). With these considerations, it is clear that Kochy had a realistic understanding of human tendencies.[2]

Perhaps the most famous philosophical ideas attributed to Kochy are a set of sayings which are best captured in the following narrative from Wolof oral tradition compiled by David P. Gamble:

> They said, he (i.e., Kochy) had three tufts (of hair). The three tufts were secret to him, he would not agree to tell anyone, except for his wife.
>
> One was called 'a king is not a relative.'
> That one 'love your wife, but do not trust her (with your secrets)'
> That one, 'an old man is good in the country.'
>
> Then, however, the king heard about it, and asked around, until he called the wife, and said, I want you to tell me the tufts of Kochy what are their names.
>
> The wife told him,
> This one, 'a king is not a relative.'
> This one, 'love your wife, but do not trust her.'
> This one, 'an old man is good in the country.'
>
> So, the king, at once, assembled all of the people of the kingdom. When they came, he called Kochy and said:
>
> "Now that I know (the meaning of) his tufts, and will kill you now (for being disrespectful), all the elders of the town came to intercede for him."

He (Kochy) said, yes, I want to tell you, king, what I said, was it not the truth? For the king had been my friend, but today, as soon as he knows my secrets, he wants to kill me. My wife, if you see I told her it, I should not have trusted her, but you see she went and told him about it, now the elders came and knelt down to intercede for me, that is why he let me go.[3]

Notes

1 Tijan M. Sallah, *Wolof* (New York: The Rosen Publishing Group, 1996), 24-25.
2 The information from the preceding five paragraphs came from author's transcription and translation of a recording of Elhadji Ndongo Faal of Njonge Faal, Louga, Senegal, who is a descendant of Kochy Barma. It should be noted that the Gambian English spelling of Kochy's last name, "Faal," is used as opposed to the Senegalese French spelling which is "Fall."
3 David P. Gamble, "Elementary Wolof Grammar" (Brisbane, CA: Gambian Studies no. 25, unpublished, 1991), 84-85.

CHAPTER 4

JOLA VERBAL ARTS OF SENEGAMBIA: A QUESTION IN SEARCH OF A LITERATURE

The Jola (Diola in French) peoples of the Casamance, Senegal, and The Gambia, are among the most resistant to the forces of Westernization (and thereby Christianization) and Arabization (and thereby Islamization) in the Senegambian region. The Jola are the dominant ethnic group in the Casamance region of Senegal and the Fogni region of The Gambia. In both Senegal and The Gambia, the Jola are a marginalized people, with very little voice in the central government. Their entrenched immersion in African traditional religions and their resistance to Westernization and Arabization has tended to compound their isolation and marginalization, especially in the modern order where these two forces confer advantages in terms of a broadening of alliances. The only major symbol of Jola empowerment came with the military seizure of presidential power in July 1994, by Yahya Jammeh in The Gambia, who came from an ethnic minority, the Jola, and who sought to reinvent history by trying to alter the social order to privilege the Jola, with only transient success. This essay will explore the verbal arts of the Jola, collections of which is scant, and explore whether there is a Jola literature and/or orature and how that links with the Jola culture of marginality.

This essay looks into the following questions: Who are the Jola peoples of West Africa? How have past narratives, mostly colonial in nature, treated them? How do the Jola see themselves? Given the paucity of written material on them, especially in English (perhaps because the Jola are latecomers to modernization), do the Jola have any tradition of literature or orature? And how has the political status of the Jola in The Gambia and in Senegal reflected a position of marginality, which in turn got reflected in their narratives? For that, we will look at the poems of the Jola woman-prophet, Aline Sitoe Jatta of Kabrousse, Casamance, and her verses of resistance against French colonialism.

Perspectives on the Jola: Who Are They?

The Jola peoples of Casamance, Senegal; Fogni, The Gambia, and Guinea Bissau are among the least studied ethnic groups of Africa. The Jola today number about 1.1 million people and constitute about 5 percent of the population of Senegal (about 810,000); 11 percent of the population of The Gambia (about 224,700); and 2 percent of the population of Guinea Bissau (38,000). The Jola should not be confused with the "Dyula" or "Jula" peoples of West Africa, who are Mande-speaking peoples who engage in petty trading across West Africa. The Jola, on the other hand, are predominantly farmers, mostly swampland rice cultivators and now also include peanut farmers. Although relatively small in number, the Jola are internally a diverse ethnic group, comprising about 16 mutually unintelligible dialects. These include Jola Fogni (or Filham); Jola Kombo; Jola Casa; Jola Huluf; Jola Kuwataye; Jola Er or Her; Jola Esulalu; Jola Banjial; Jola Jiamat or Feloup; Jola Calequisse; Jola Hulon; Jola Fogni Buluf; Jola Blis, Jola Karon (Karoninka); Jola Bayot; and Jola Bainunka.[1]

In the colonial narratives, the ancestors of the Jolas are usually described as "Feloups" or "Flups" or "Banyons." Colonial narratives about the Jola have been uncongratulatory. In narrative after narrative, they view the Jola with tainted binoculars, with an implicit bias that is patently self-congratulating, that involve measuring the Jola against their own externally imposed colonial metric. Their narratives represent attempts, perhaps unwittingly, to "put down" an entire people and not to see and to understand them within their own context. The colonial syllogism went like this, the British wear suits. Suits are marks of civilization. But the Jola wear only a piece of cloth to cover their private parts; so, the Jola were a significant standard deviation from the British or French norm; hence they must then be "uncivilized." This way of reasoning, of course, is problematic because the British and French live in countries where there is cold weather, but the Jola live in a generally hot climate. In narrative after narrative, colonial writers portray the Jola as a meagerly clothed, primitive people without kings or queens, and without any system of hierarchical government. In fact, in many narratives the Jola are described as "acephalous," as without a hierarchical leader or head. Francis Moore, in his *Travels Into the Inland Parts of Africa* (1723), described the Jola (in this case, the Feloups) in condescending detail. He noted that the Jola did not have any institutions of centralized rule and were therefore difficult to pacify:

> On the South-side of this River (The Gambia River) over against James Fort, in the Empire of Fonia (*a reference to Fogni*, italics mine) and but a little Way inland, are a Sort of People called Floops, who are in a manner wild. They border close to the Mundigoes (*Mandingoes*, italics mine) and are bitter Enemies to each other. Their Country is of a vast Extent, but they have no King among them, each of their Towns being fortified with Sticks drove all round, and filled up with Clay. They are independent of each other, and under the Government of no one Chief, notwithstanding which, they unite fo firmly, that all the Force of the Mandingoes (tho' fo very numerous) cannot get the better of them. [2]

Moore's colonial narrative is heavily influenced by the colonial agenda of divide and rule. The narrative is blatantly suspect, for why should the enmity between the Jola and the Mandingo be of interest, except that it reflects colonial propensity to find differences so that they can be exploited to sow division and to gain advantage? Moore goes on further to give a psychological assessment of the Jola, describing them as practicing retributive justice but as compassionate if treated kindly. He noted, "These Floops have the Character never to forgive, or let the least Injury go unrevenged, but then, to make amends, the least good Office done them is always repaid by them with a grateful Acknowledgement."[3]

Henry Fenwick Reeve, colonial governor of the Gambia from 1900 to 1911, in his book, *The Gambia: Its History, Ancient, Medieval and Modern* (1969), also offers an unflattering perspective about the Jola.

> The Flups .... Those who inhabit the mouth of the river Zamanee (the Kazamansa) on the northside (the country towards the Gambia) are extremely savage, with whom no nation have any commerce. Everyone has his own god, according to his particular fancy; one worships a bullock's horn; another a beast, or a tree, to whom they sacrifice in their manner.[4]

The Jola are described here as "savage" and practicing various forms of animism. Reeve gives further description of the Jola:

> Their dress is like the negroes of Cape de Verde and the inhabitants of the river Gambia, which consists in a piece of cloth, striped according to the custom of the country, which barely covers their privities. They have no succession of kings, the most absolute and powerful amongst them bearing sway. They cultivate their land in pretty good order, which they sow with millet and rice. Their riches consist of bullocks, cows and goats, of which many of them have great droves. Their villages are well peopled, distant from each other about a quarter of a league.[5]

Here again, we learn from Reeve's description that the Jola ran primitive, independent, populous, and acephalous communities that were geographically dispersed, where the law of survival of the strongest prevailed. This was buttressed by the fact that the

Jola were good farmers and self-sufficient who lived in harmony with their ecosystem and had abundant natural wealth.

Reeve goes on to give a description of the physical and attitudinal characteristics of the Jola in lurid, if not graphic, condescending detail:

> The Felupp negroes, who occupy... on the banks of the Cazamance, and on the upper part of the river Vintam, retain all the rudeness of savage life, in which they delight to live and remain, without, however, being of a ferocious character. The country they inhabit is well covered, and fertile: they rear cattle, which they defend with great courage against lions, leopards and bears, which are common in their forests.
>
> The Felupps go almost naked; they wear only a little apron passed between the thighs;... they bind the upper arms, wrists, upper parts of thighs, above the knees, and the upper and lower parts of the legs, with leather laces, so that the intervals between the parts of their limbs thus bound are much larger than in the natural state.
>
> They cicatrise their face and body, and engrave on them all sorts of irregular and ludicrous figures.
>
> These negroes have very wooly and curled hair, but longer that of negroes in general. They collect it on top of their head, and over their forehead, where they form it into a sort of queue, or aigrette, which stands erect to the height of five or six inches; they let their beard grow, which they collect and tie, so that it forms a point projecting several inches from the chin.
>
> They cover themselves with Gri-gris (charms); their colour is deep black; their skin is rough, their features tolerably regular, and resemble those of the blacks of India rather than that of the negroes.
>
> The Felupps are small and chubby, but strong and active; their physiognomy is downcast, and they are reserved. They have but little communication with their neighbors, and they are very jealous of their women, who nevertheless are not pretty.
>
> Their arms wear bows and poisoned arrows, with four or five lances held in the same hand as the bow, while their arrows were swung in two quivers over their back, one at each

shoulder, by which one would conclude they were ambidextrous.

...Although, they are savage, melancholy, and not very communicative, their neighbors do not complain of them, and the Felupps pass for good people; they are, however, warlike, and when offended, they avenge themselves with ferocity.

It would be curious to inquire into the origin of this horde, whose characteristic features, forms, manners and customs differ considerably from those of the nations by which they are surrounded.

...The direct descendants of the Floops of former chroniclers still exist in a nation called by us the Jolahs, the Banyons, a branch of the Floops occupying Combo....[6]

Reeve's reference to "Cazamance" is today's "Casamance" and "Vintam" is today's "Bintang Creek"—a tributary of the Gambia River. Although Reeve's description is tinged with colonial condescension, it opens us to aspects of the Jola past which has been carried into the present: that the Jola are hardworking, agricultural peoples who practice traditional African religions; who are peaceful until when offended (after which they can be ferocious fighters); who are reserved, not garrulous and therefore guardedly secretive; who in the past carried body tattoos or skin scarring and had hairdos resembling the African-American TV character, Mr. T; who are jealously protective of their women; and who seem to live apart from their other ethnic neighbors.

Reeve, in a later description of the Jola, notes:

> ...the Banyons still exist in small communities, and are mostly employed in the collection of palm oil, palm wine, and kernels, with other forest products. The Jolahs, however, are still a distinct people occupying the same territory as in the time of the Portuguese, still known as Fogni. They are comparatively short in stature, plump and well formed, with pleasant dreamy faces, round heads, with the tuft of hair like a Red Indian's scalp lock still in evidence. They still despise clothing to a degree, even in the streets of Bathurst (colonial name for Banjul, Gambia's capital), and wear ligatures round their limbs and bodies.[7]

These colonial narratives are self-servingly amusing, if not self-aggrandizing; they reflected the asymmetrical power of the colonial monologue in their encounter with the "native" other; they reflect a problematic imperial pattern—that only the bowler-hatted colonial intruder "knows" and "speaks"; but the "native" has to be silent. The self-apprehension of the "native" is never factored into the narrative. To get a balanced and contrasting perspective, however, it is important to explore in the next section how the Jola see themselves; to ask the question-- do the Jola have any literature or orature? One needs to also ask, how do their self-apprehension and narratives relate to their own marginality?

Although it is difficult to point to any distinct text that represents the existence of a Jola literature, the Jola do have a rich orature (the vast majority of which is not yet recorded) which characterize and enrich Jola life and attitude to the world. It is important to place this orature within the broader self-affirming narratives of how the Jola see themselves--- outside of the condescending, biased gaze, the intermittent cultural voyeurism, of the colonial intruder. It is important to note that Jola life is defined by work and by leisure in the form of rituals and ceremonies which characterize different rites of passage.

Jola Life and the Jola Cultural Self-apprehension:

Every Jola belongs to an extended family household that lives in a compound known as *fank*. The *fank*, by the principle of subsidiarity, is the lowest level of decision-making in Jola society, headed by the father. The Jola are patriarchal. (Personal Interview).[8]

Jola life is defined by birth, circumcision, marriage, religion, and death. The Jola do not celebrate birthdays as significant ceremonies. When a baby is born, on the eighth day, a naming ceremony is held which is called *kuliye* (which resembles the Mandinka word, *kuliyoo*, used for a naming ceremony in which there is cutting of the baby's hair). Every member of the community shares in the joy of the new arrival. (It is possible that this ceremony is borrowed from the Mandinka—as the Jola have had a long history of interactions with the Mandinka, in which the Mandinka tried to subjugate and convert them to Islam, but often met with fierce resistance. They have fought interethnic wars and made peace and sometimes even intermarried.) If the family has means, they may slaughter a ruminant, such as a bull, sheep, or a goat, or even another animal such as a pig or chicken (depending on the means of a family) may be killed and its meat cooked to entertain guests at the naming celebration. If, however, a family is totally without means, they may hold a "small" naming ceremony, but will call it a *nyambuwe* which should lower the expectations of guests, implying that the event will be a very modest one. (Personal Interview)[9]

Another important rite of passage that a Jola boy or young man goes through is known as *futampaf*. A *futampaf* is held every fifteen to thirty years for young men and it is a ceremony in which they are taken to the bush for two weeks and taught lessons about what it means to be responsible men. Young men are taught about how to handle themselves well in society and the role of an adult. Usually, the oldest men speak and share wisdom about life, based on events, issues, and/or disputes that have risen in the past and how they were resolved by their forefathers. At the *futampaf*, there is a reliance on learning from precedence and from age-old practices.

In a *futampaf*, all of the Jolas in the various communities are invited. Uncles and aunts of the young men going through the *futampaf* are also invited and given special accommodation and treatment. For every young man participating, a bull is slaughtered and the meat cooked to entertain the guests during the festivities. A bull is also killed for every uncle and aunt participating. This makes the *futampaf* a very expensive ceremony and families participating have to plan and to save resources for it in advance. (Personal Interview)[10]

An important ceremony for women is *ebunee*, which is a retreat held annually or biannually to work on a particular topic (*waaf*). A woman is chosen to be in charge of a project and to provide progress report and feedback. Jola women from far and near attend the retreat, which usually lasts from one to two weeks, and there are discussions on various self-help activities and enterprises, and there are also festivities of song and dance. In an *ebunee*, the women gathered also choose one woman as "queen," but this queen is only ceremonial and has no royal powers. The queen chosen is only for recognition and reigns for only one or two years until the next *ebunee*. (Personal Interview)[11]

The Jola are very insular in their marriage choices—a Jola should marry only a Jola, once young men and women reach puberty or marriage age. Men can marry their nieces, and women—their nephews. This is done to strengthen ethnic cultural ties and to ensure that differences during marriage can be easily mediated. As a result, Jolas have very few divorces. Marriage choices are usually made by the father of the suitor. Jolas do not allow dating. Generally, young men follow their father's wishes and pose few challenges to their father's authority. For the young women, virginity is a premium. The Jola guard virginity seriously. A promiscuous young woman is deemed to bring shame to her family. (Personal Interview)[12]

When a marriage is proposed, usually the father of the suitor gives a "bull" or "cow" as the bride's price, as well as other livestock to be used to buy special dresses for the bride's mother and father, and bride's brothers. When the marriage takes place, all of the elders in the village gather to pray for the newly married couple. The young men in the village are advised to stay away from the newly married woman, since she now has a husband. (Personal Interview)[13]

The Jola traditionally practice polygamy. Marriage is based on socioeconomic status, and so the larger the farms and livestock a man possesses, the more they are inclined to marry more wives to bear them children to help them with farm labor. In earlier days, when there was little mechanized farming, having more family labor was particularly handy. With a large family, they are able to cultivate food crops such as rice, maize, millet, sorghum, and some peanuts which they can sell to get money to buy manufactured goods and pay taxes. (Personal Interview)[14]

The Jola celebrate with a wide range of masquerades and musical performances-- one of the most popular masquerade being the *ekumpai*. The *ekumpai* is a masked dancer usually dressed with dried palm leaves in the shape of a spruce with a sharp projectile protruding from its head. Usually, it will be accompanied by a crowd of drummers, dancers, and singers. The *ekumpai* would then dance by sticking its projectile on to the earth and swirling its head and the rest of the body in a roundabout manner in a circle, like a leafy porcupine. The name *ekumpai* derives from *kumpo*, which literally means "one does not know who the individual is;" in short, it points to a rite of secrecy, a cryptic ritual. (Personal Interview)[15]

The other Jola masquerade is the *samai*. The *samai* is a masked dancer who is dressed with discarded rice bags or gunny sacks. Like the *ekumpai*, the *samai* is accompanied by drummers, dancers, and singers. Another Jola masked dancer is the *kankurang* who is dressed with the red bark of tree, head to knee, and barks are also tied into rings around the leg of the masked dancer. Usually, the *kankurang* will dance with a cutlass in one hand and stamp the feet on the ground in several fast, repetitive motions, accompanied by a rhythmic drum, singers, and clappers. (Personal Interview)[16]

One of the activities that accompany festivities is communal street drumming called *bugaraab* or *bukarabu*. Usually, in a *bugaraab*, a skilled drummer (*ajaalao*) will play multiple drums, usually three, simultaneously. The drums will be made from hollowed-out tree trunks and animal skin, and will be of different sizes so that they give different sounds. The bigger the trunk of the tree is, the bigger the sound. In a *bugaraab*, the Jola community dances and makes merry for up to six hours nonstop. Through it, children run around and have fun, and elders—men and women—interact, dance, and make gestures, sometimes carrying freshlycut palm leaves or mango tree branches, daintily waving them toward the sky. (Personal Interview)[17]

In addition to entertainment activities, the Jola also celebrate funerals as a sad chapter in a person's life. When a person dies, before the person is buried, an old person is brought from within the family to talk to the dead person. In that conversation, the dead person is asked to tell them about what happened in the person's life to result in their death. Because the Jola believe in witchcraft, the conversation with the dead is believed to reveal whether the person died of natural causes or perished from the spell of a witch. (Personal Interview)[18]

Before the dead person is buried, the Jola usually have a three-day ceremony. During that period, the dead body is embalmed with traditional herbs to prevent it from rotting and from smelling. The body is then transported on a stretcher by six strong men to each home in the community to say good-bye. If there is a home the dead body does not want to go, the spirit of the dead body will enter the six men carrying the stretcher, and they will be seen struggling and the body carriers would then ignore that home. If it is a home that the dead body wants to go to, the body carriers would proceed smoothly to that home. After the processions and a three-day festival, the dead person is buried with some of their artifacts of greatest value, such as their gun, spear, arrows, and sword. (Personal Interview)[19]

During the funeral ceremony, there are special people or helpers called *assempulao* who are usually the nieces or nephews of the dead person. The *assempulao* have a special place in Jola society as they are given broad degrees of freedom to act. They do the domestic chores, mediate family matters, can slaughter chicken in the compound and cook them to entertain guests, and generally have broad latitude to act to entertain guests. They can be resourceful with any assets in the compound and use them as they wish to entertain guests without anyone complaining. (Personal Interview)[20]

Jola life aside, do the Jola have a literature and/or orature? From the available evidence, there does not seem to exist any distinctive text that one can point to suggest that they have a literature; however, there is a rich existing orature. In terms of their orature, there are three strands of oral narratives that can be identified: (1) stories (singular, *kerigeg;* plural *uregawu*); (2) poems/songs (*kechimak*); and (3) proverbs (*mansali*). In storytelling, usually by older folk, children gather at their feet and the storyteller holds them spellbound with stories about animals and about their hair-raising adventures. Various animals are identified with particular traits, such as cunning with rabbits/hares and greed with hyenas. Often the motif is to teach a moral, such as greed does not pay or lying can result in punishment. The children are then taught good principles about how to live well in society. The storyteller among the Jola is called *arigawo*. The singer is called *uchimao*. (Personal Interview)[21]

A few examples of Jola stories (*uregawu*) are as follows: The first story is "The Hyena and the Rabbit." The story goes:

> A farmer working on his farm saw a rabbit and set a trap. He caught the rabbit alive and took it home. At his home, he tied the rabbit on a tree near his goat, and went out to work. A hyena came wanting to eat the goat and asked the rabbit, "Can we trade places?" The rabbit agreed. The hyena untied the rabbit, and the rabbit tied the hyena near the goat. The hyena ate the goat, but was unable to untie himself. When the farmer came, he found the hyena and was outraged at what he did. He killed the hyena. (Personal Interview)[22]

The motif of the story is that excessive greed is bad for you. It could even kill you.

Another *kerigeg* (story) of the Jola titled, "Jealousy Does Not Pay," goes like this:

> There were two women married to one man and each had a son. One son was very successful. He had left the village and gone very far and worked to make something for himself. He came back to the village with bags full of money and plenty of goods. The mother of the other son saw this and was jealous. He saw that her son had stayed home and was playful. He had no focus and no direction. So one day, he ordered her son. "Don't bring disgrace to me. Please go as far as you can and do as well as your step brother did!" The young man listened to her mother's orders and left without any plan or preparation. He ended up being killed at his new destination to the anguish of his distraught mother. (Personal Interview)[23]

The moral of this story is that, whatever one does in life, one should plan and prepare for it. Following other's successes wildly could lead to one's own peril.

The second strand of Jola oratures are poems/songs (*kechimak*). Poems/songs are used for both sacred and secular rituals. To understand their use in the context of the sacred, it is important to note that Jola religion is decentralized into several spirit shrines and fetishes to which a family or families owe their devotion. Usually, the spirit shrine is a sacred grove in the bush to which the family engages the mysteries of nature. In engagement with spirits, the Jola use poetry to implore the spirits to bring peace, rain, and natural prosperity to their farms. Perhaps one of the most engaging narratives about Jola religion is one presented by Robert M. Baum in his ritually rich book on the Jola woman- prophet, Aline Sitoe Jatta (in French, Alinesitowe Diatta), titled, *West Africa's Women of God* (2016).[24] Aline was born in 1920, in Kabrousse, Lower Casamance, and passed away on May 22, 1944, in Timbuktu, Mali.[25] She was born as an orphan among the Esulalu Jolas and raised by her uncle Elubaliin Jatta (*In Praise of Black*, 60).[26] She was a symbol of Senegalese resistance against French colonial authority which resulted in her exile to Timbuktu, Mali. Her short but truly consequential life earned her the heroic sobriquet as the Senegalese "Jola, Joan of Arc."[27]

In her youth, Aline left her village of Kabrousse for the French seat of "white power" in Ziguinchor, Senegal. When she discovered Ziguinchor as only a marginal colonial outpost, she proceeded to the real seat of colonial power in Dakar and got exposed to several unfamiliar landscapes along the way.[28] In Dakar, she dwelled in the Medina (the squatter settlements by migrants from all over Senegal) that had developed outside the white seat of power.[29] Although illiterate, she experienced in Dakar the humiliations and frustrations suffered by the natives under colonialism. Her experiences magnified her boldness to join the resistance and to seek redress.[30] Dakar, in short, proved to be a source of education to Aline about what was wrong with colonialism.

When she returned to her home region of Casamance, she had a revelation, a calling from the ancestors. Simone Schwarz-Bart noted:

> On her way home, approaching Casamance, she heard a vague call and hurried her step. Once in Kabrousse, her mouth suddenly opened to speak with the voices of the ancestors, the *Boekin*, who spoke through her the truth about humanity's problems and the world's problems, but then began to speak about the problems of the Diola people./These words healed the sick and desperate; these words told the future. Day and night, coming from all corners of Casamance, people flocked to her to witness this miracle. Already her reputation was growing and crossing borders. People came to see her from Kaolack, Saint Louis, Guinea Bissau, and even from far off Mauretania. They may have sought healing from an obsolete illness or from an ill spirit possessing the body. Above all, they wanted to hear from the very mouth of the prophet the words that foretold the future.[31]

Aline became a Jola "prophet" whose fame spread wide and far in the immediate West Africa region. Her shrine of *Houssahara* became a popular site of pilgrimage to the Jola supreme deity, *Emitai*. Although the Jolas have an enduring tradition of "prophets" or of "messengers of God"-- for which they use the epithet *Emitai dabognol*, prophetic tradition used to be confined only to men.[32] After colonialism, this shifted to mostly women, and Aline became a pioneer in that regard among the esulalu Jolas. Her teachings about Jola religion (the *Awasena* path) involved instructions from *Emitai* and from the rituals that needed to be performed to supplicate the desires of the deities and to appease the supreme deity. The rituals often involved sacrifice of a black bull and some pigs and chickens, which the entire community ate together over several days, accompanied by songs or poems honoring the ancestors. The prophetic tradition continued as other women followed Aline's steps by developing priviliged communication with the supreme deity and engaging in the *kasila* ritual, a community ritual seeking rain from the supreme deity.[33]

When the French, in 1937, prohibited the Jola from the cultivation of upland rice (a drought resilient food crop) in the Lower Casamance region, and instead promoted its replacement with peanuts (a cash crop), Aline challenged the French and encouraged the Jola to continue to grow rice, the staple. Besides, she saw in French policy, a pernicious motivation, which was purely to serve their industrial interests while simultaneously ignoring the immediate food security and welfare needs of the Jola community. Although Aline was aware of the metropolitan power of the French against the Jola's marginal situation, she was also conscious of the power of populist resistance. She saw in peanut cultivation destructive tendencies which degraded forests and also led to the loss of biodiversity, such as of important sources of palm products and wild fruits, herbal medicine, and game.[34] A poem by a significant Jola priest of *Ehugna* captures this local dilemma:

> The young Balibah (a title for Alinesitoue)
> The young Balibah and her child.
> Ohoway, Ohoway.
> Who is looking for upland rice.
> Young Balibah, who gave us our rice[35]

The poem or song is simple, but it captures the vigor of Aline and her advocacy of Jola survival interest in growing rice.

Aline's populist, spiritual power grew, as large numbers of Jola pilgrims came to Kabrousse to hear her teachings and to carry back to their places of origin the charity and rites of *kasila*. She greeted them and provided them with accommodation and fed the pilgrims with the meat from past sacrifices for almost a week. They will eat all the meat outside for it was forbidden to bring the sacrificed meat inside. Aline would take various gifts brought by pilgrims— baskets of rice and fruit as well as the black chickens and black bulls and palm wine and perform the *huasene* at her shrine in *Houssahara*, asking *Emitai* to provide them with help,[36] and it appeared that *Emitai* would answer her prayers in the form of rainfall for their farms and cures of various ailments. Her prayers for the pilgrims were followed by the ritual of the *nyakul* and the *djigum*, which were dances for the women fertility shrine.[37] Usually, when they do the *Kasila* ritual and had the communal meals, the gathering would perform a dance and sing Aline's songs until late at night. The song or poem goes:

> Kasila ho!
> Ata-Emit ho!
> We are tired.
> Emitai will send rain.[38]

After the pilgrimage, the Jola pilgrims carried cow's horns stuffed with the sacred soil from Aline's shrine which they carried home to start their own shrines.[39]

In addition to being a "prophet," Aline was a social change agent and a poet. She challenged hierarchy and advocated egalitarian ideals across gender and age.[40] In a poignantly resonant poem, which illustrates her struggle for social justice against the domineering forces of the French, she proclaimed an egalitarian spirituality:

> All the women of the family have said
> That an idiot has taken charge of the fetish
> There it is, very happy
> All of a sudden, we hear the thunder high in the sky.
> We are all in a great hurry to take our canoe.
> The French are approaching.
> There it is that the rice is thrown all over the place
> There is the bird that flew high up between the clouds and the sky.
> Oh! God! Pardon us.
> Give us water, thanks to our "charity"
> Because the French have plunged us
> into famine.[41]

The village republican spirit of the religion of Aline is reflected in the lines that "an idiot has taken charge of the fetish." The fetish did not need "priests"—but that even a member of the "laity"—that even an "idiot," an ordinary person can perform the ritual. Baum describes it well that "Even an idiot can carry their prayers to *Emitai*, and *Emitai* will respond with life-giving rain."[42]

Another poem by Aline postulates the revolutionary resistance of the Jola "natives" against the coercive machinations of the French Empire.[43] As peanut farming spread, Aline saw this as a trap that the French had set for her people which would destroy Jola lives and make them dependent on the colonial economy. She saw peanut farming, according to Father Diamacoune Senghor of Casamance interpretations, as the "farming of people who are not free."[44] In a sense, her own poetry was beginning to reflect her struggles between the colonial intrusion and reordering of local priorities and the native resistance to such agenda setting. Her poem captures these sentiments:

> I am very happy to show how you must take it,
> To cut the neck of a steer
> Because I regret to see the Europeans kill people with their long rifles.
> A day will come when God will inflict a harsh punishment upon Them.
> Because that which they do is not good
> And God does not like evil-doers.[45]

During the Second World War years, the French Vichy administration intensified their imperial efforts in the Esulalu and throughout the Casamance region. The Jola experienced a social crisis characterized by proselytization to join the Catholic Church, as well as "taxation, conscription, …and drought."[46] The French intensified efforts not only to conquer the minds and the territorial space of the Jola, but also to win their hearts to Catholicism. As a result, Jola society was divided—between those who staunchly defended the old religion of *awassena* and those who aligned with French Catholic belief. Aline, a devout advocate of the old religion, was seen as a threat to French interests so she was arrested on November 11, 1942.[47] The administrator of Casamance at the time was Commander Sajous who was based in Zinguinchor and who commanded the Jolas to hand over their rice reserves as contribution to the war effort. Aline resisted and publicly recited the following song/poem:

> Here comes the French
> Watch out, get ready, watch out
> Diolas, get out your rifles
> Do as the whites do
> What did we ever do to them?
> Why do they treat us this way?[48]

Asking very legitimate questions in her poem, this, however, did not win sympathies for her cause among the colonial administrators who were unprepared to grant horizontal relations and dialogue with the "native." The Vichy regime was heavy-handed and rapacious, and their local tentacles, in the form of Sajous, fetched for her immediate arrest. During her arrest, she was injured and taken for confinement at a camp in the Kayes region in eastern Senegal, and condemned to ten years in jail.[49] The charge against her was that she "led the population into systematic disobedience, and was at the origin of the Diola revolt."[50] Later, however, the French recognized that keeping her in confinement near to Casamance was a bad idea, for if nothing--- it amplified her heroism. Therefore, they secretly exiled her to Timbuktu, Mali, where she was socially cut off from contact with her community and followers. She tragically died there in prison on May 22, 1944, at the young age of twenty-four.[51]

The third strand of Jola orature are proverbs (*mansali*). Proverbs among the Jola are like language lubricants, speech-appetizers, or speech-slime, that facilitate or invigorate speech and storytelling. In fact, many Jola songs and poems are a piecing together of proverbs into a grand tapestry like the interweaving of grass in a thatched hut. Among the Jola, the proverb can be used to praise, to remember, to educate, or to insult. J. David Sapir captured some funeral verses (*bunansanab*) in a song that was performed by Anara Suleman Jeme of Jila Kunda at the funeral of Jaan Badjie obtained in 1965, from the town of Jirem in Casamance, Senegal. The verses were provided by Sapir's informant, Kalilu Badjie (Sapir website). A few proverbs from Jeme's *bunansan,* all obtained from Sapir's website,[52] would suffice as illustrations.

One of the proverbial lines in the *bunansan* was, *Abili binab busibsab jiwu kabasa, ban le bo mukuluje* translating as "Abili, the corpse is questioned and changes to a mat. And then there are no bad words." Since, as noted earlier, in Jola tradition, when a person dies, the corpse is questioned for cause of death—the good humor in this proverbial verse is that this dead person becomes "welcoming"; that is, "changes to a mat," and so what follows then is only *"good words,"* or a *"eulogy."* A second Jola proverb goes, *Batan buloe nawunen bo,* or "Bullets fall, and he turns and farts" or "Bullets fall and he shows his ass (as if to fart); that is, defies the bullet." This proverb has a dual meaning, suggesting either courage or timidity. When bullets are fired and a person turns and farts, it can either be interpreted that the person is courageous and makes a mockery of the act by "farting," or that the person is timid and the experience is so frightening that they lose all sense of control to the extent of "farting." A third Jola proverb goes, *Busanay bati Abantan o kone, inayool api manaiko mapinco banomer,* or "They say that his mother always put him in danger, for prettiness is bought with a heifer." This criticizes the custom of the "bride price for women" in which the "value" of a bride is reduced to a "bride price," when in fact other considerations should matter more both to the bride and to the suitor: such as compatibility, shared values and beliefs, and shared goals in life. A fourth Jola proverb goes, *Ajaneni nen kawonk ebeoo,* or "He is as known as his cow's call." This conflates the "owner" with his "mobile property" and suggests perhaps the popularity and familiarity of a person. A fifth Jola proverb goes, *Bukoji bunuli ujuk nen jisond,* or "Ugliness is woven when you see a thatch roof" or "Observe a thatch roof and see how ugliness is woven." This is a complex proverb and perhaps points to the intricacies of "ugliness" when one peals its tangled branches and leaves. A sixth Jola proverb, provided by Momodou Kolley, is that "A dog surveys its environment first before lying down," which suggests that people should not be careless about the safety of their environment. Considering the three different strands of orature just discussed, the Jola do have a rich and untapped body of orature that perhaps need more investigation and recording.

Marginality and the Scramble to the Center

Reflecting on the issue of "marginality," how does the Jola's peripheral position in Senegalese and Gambian society contribute to the relegation of their narratives to the margin and therefore contributed to their own marginality? It could be argued that the Jola have been latecomers to accepting Christianity and Islam and have therefore been disadvantaged in getting the privileges conferred by reading and writing in European languages and Arabic, which has given other Senegambian ethnic groups global advantage in being part of larger world co-fraternity. The empires and states built by the Arabic and by the Western intrusion tended to confer privileges to those local agents who have assimilated or adapted to the missionaries' languages, technical skills, and values of those power intrusions.

This adverse dynamic on the Jola has, however, been increasingly changing in the past fifty years, as more Jola became Moslem or Christian and sent their children to Moslem and to Western schools. Successes, particularly in Western schools, has made the Jola successful professionals and in some cases to contest for political power at the central governments of The Gambia and Senegal. In recent years, there has been a Jola president, ministers, doctors, engineers, and other professionals. The association of "Jola" with the work of "housemaids" in the households of other ethnic groups (to the extent that the word "Jola" became an epithet for "housemaid) is drastically and justifiably disappearing. This is all for the good. There is little reason to justify the subjugation of an entire ethnic group simply because they initially preferred keeping their traditions and were resistant to modernizing forces.

Already in agriculture, the Jola, as an ethnic group, contribute a lot to the Senegalese and Gambian economy. They are already contributing and will contribute more to other areas of Senegambian society also. One of Senegal's most famous architects, Pierre Goudiaby Atepa, is a Jola, who was born in Baila, Casamance, and studied engineering at Rensselaer Polytechnic Institute. He is credited with designing major architectural marvels, such as the African Renaissance Monument in Dakar, the Central Bank of West African States headquarters, the Yundum National Airport of the Gambia, the ECOWAS (Economic Community of West African States) head office in Lome, Togo, Place de La Nation in Chad, and many of the African continent's most significant architectural landmarks.[53]

Another significant Jola personality of world repute—though in this case adverse—is the Gambia's former president, Yahya Jemus Junkung Jammeh. Jammeh was born in Kanilai in 1965, in the Fogni region in the Gambia of a career wrestler-father and a trader-mother. He joined the army after completing high school, had a year's military training at Fort McClellan in the United States, and was at the rank of sergeant when he carried out a military coup against the democratic government of Sir Dawda Kairaba Jawara on July 22, 1994. In his initial years, Jammeh became the chairman of the Armed Forces Provisional Ruling Council (AFPRC), broke relations with mainland China, and aligned the country with, and received money from, Taiwan, and used this and other resources to pursue a number of ambitious infrastructure projects to gain public credibility (built the national airport, started the first university, built a monument in the form of an arch as one enters Banjul—the capital city, and expanded the road network and hospitals significantly). However, these positive initial moves were short lived and got overshadowed by his negatives as he outmaneuvered and removed his other four junior army coup coconspirators, eliminated political opponents, undermined inherited political institutions, muzzled the political opposition, persecuted the press, and perpetuated a regime of terror and fear. He carried out elections amid a paralyzed opposition and crowned himself president in successive national elections and perpetuated a culture of patronage and a personality cult throughout the country, with large pictures of himself posted on billboards in main thoroughfares and even in nonpublic buildings. He also had his antics of claiming he can cure HIV-AIDS and performed therapies on patients (when the international scientific consensus had not found a cure yet), and of making anti-colonial and anti-imperialist rantings. Most damaging to the country, he became rapaciously corrupt, seizing local properties and appropriating some for himself and plundering the country's resources to acquire a vast wealth alleged to be over $1 billion with properties in the Middle East, North Africa, United States, Europe, and elsewhere.[54]

During his rule, Jammeh tried to change The Gambia's social and cultural order by privileging the Jola with key political appointments and key positions in business. This perhaps may have been justified as restitution for historical disadvantages suffered by the Jola. He hosted annually an International Roots Festival in his hometown of Kanilai, cleverly exploiting the celebration of the African-American author Alex Haley's genealogical trace of his Gambian "Roots" and used that global platform to feature prominently Jola musical and dance arts and the *futampaf* ceremony. The attempt to popularize the *futampaf* and other Jola celebratory rituals reflected how culture can be reinvented and reordered when political power rests in the hands of marginalized ethnic groups.

This essay has explored the question of whether the Jola have a literature and/or orature and concluded that, on the basis of the available evidence, one could not point to any example of a corpus of literature, but one could point, undoubtedly, to a rich and widely undocumented orature, which needs further exploration and recording. This essay studied those oral "literary" forms and provided examples, including the poetry of that hero of Jola resistance against French colonialism, the prophet Aline Sitoe Jatta of Kabrousse Casamance. We have also explored colonial derogatory perceptions of the Jola, using their own externally imposed biased metric, and juxtaposed that with the Jola's own affirmative self-apprehension. We have argued that the Jola position of marginality in the modern order in The Gambia and in Senegal was linked to their resistance to Westernization and to Arabization and their strong loyalty to their indigenous culture. This situation is, however, changing, as more Jola acquire Western Christian and Arabo-Islamic schooling and values, and reap the benefits of modernity conferred by those encounters. We discussed two famous Jola personalities in the modern era, who have reaped these benefits of modernity, Pierre Goudiaby Atepa, a continentally acclaimed architect from Senegal, and Yahya Jemus Junkung Jammeh, The Gambia's former authoritarian president.

Notes

1 J. David Sapir, *A Grammmar of Diola-Fogny* (Cambridge: Cambridge University Press, 1965), xiv-xv, 1-2.
2 Francis Moore, *Travels into the Inland Parts of Africa* (London: Henry and Cave, 1730), 25.
3 Ibid., 26.
4 Henry Fenwick Reeve, *The Gambia: Its History, Ancient, Medieval and Modern* (New York: Negro Universities Press, 1969), 190
5 Ibid.
6 Ibid., 191-93.
7 Ibid., 193.
8 Momodou Kolley, *Personal Interview* by Phone on the Jola, January 2019.
9 Ibid.
10 Ibid.
11 Ibid.
12 Ibid.
13 Ibid.
14 Ibid.
15 Ibid.
16 Ibid.
17 Ibid.
18 Ibid.
19 Ibid.
20 Ibid.
21 Ibid.
22 Ibid.
23 Ibid.

24 Richard M. Baum, *West Africa's Women of God* (Bloomington and Indianapolis: Indiana University Press, 2016).
25 Simone Schwarz-Bart, *In Praise of Black Women (*Madison: The University of Wisconsin Press, 2003),68-72.
26 Ibid., 60.
27 Baum, *West Africa's Women of God*, 2.
28 Schwarz-Bart, *In Praise of Black Women*, 60.
29 Ibid., 62.
30 Ibid., 63.
31 Ibid., 64.
32 Baum, *West Africa's Women of God*, 1-5.
33 Ibid., 1-2.
34 Ibid., 145.
35 Ibid., 144.
36 Ibid.,146-47.
37 Ibid, 147.
38 Ibid.
39 Ibid.
40 Ibid., 166.
41 Ibid.
42 Ibid.
43 Ibid., 170.
44 Ibid., 168.
45 Ibid., 170.
46 Ibid., 171.
47 Schwarz-Bart, *In Praise of Black Women*,70.
48 Ibid.
49 Ibid., 71.
50 Ibid., 71.
51 Ibid., 71-72.
52 J. David Sapir website, University of Virginia, Anthropology, Kujamaat Language and Folklore Materials.
53 Nduta Waweru, "Meet Pierre Atepa Goudiaby, The Senegalese Architect Behind the Most Prolific Landmarks in Africa," *Face2Face Africa* (September 3, 2018).
54 Stuart A. Reid, "The Dictators Who Love America," *The Atlantic* (February 8, 2016); Lamin Jahateh, "Recovery of Jammeh's 'Stolen Assets' Would Take Years," The Point, Banjul, Gambia (July 14, 2017); Abdoulaye Saine, The Paradox of Third-wave Democratization in Africa (Lanham, MD: Lexington Books, 2009).

CHAPTER 5

THE NEW GAMBIAN POETS AND THEIR POETRY

In the contemporary Gambian poetic scene—particularly in the post-2000 period—few poets have risen to merit critical attention. The body of Gambian literature is limited, and many of its significant accomplishments are by exiled writers such as the late Ebou Dibba, Sally Singhateh, and myself. Since there were no universities in The Gambia until 1999 (because of the lack of visionary political leadearship), many of these writers had to go abroad for further education and eventually stayed in their host countries. The political climate in The Gambia also did not help. The advent of a Yahya Jammeh-led coup d'état in 1994 brought in an authoritarian government that trampled on civil liberties, including the press and any critical writing. This dictatorship lasted until 2016, when Gambians mustered courage and mobilized for his peaceful ouster through the ballot box and elected President Adama Barrow. Over these years, there were few literary publications. With the exception of a short-lived literary magazine called *Ndanaan* in the seventies, and *Topic Magazine* in the nineties, Gambian writers had few outlets. The occasional poem appeared in newspapers like the *Gambian Observer* and *Foroyaa*, but none were trailblazers. In short, a combination of a lagging educational system, limited civil liberties, and an embryonic literary infrastructure resulted in a literary community largely amateur in its technical, stylistic, and thematic accomplishments. In spite of these challenges, the poets Mariama Khan, Momodou Sallah, and Bala S. K. Saho have emerged as promising new Gambian voices of this generation.

Khan was born in Brikama Newtown, The Gambia, to a Senegalese father and a Gambian mother. Her father was a prolific writer, whether it was meticulously recording his everyday transactions or writing letters in French or in *Ajami* (Wolof written in Arabic script) to family back home. Her mother encouraged her to take on writing roles, having her act as the women's group scribe and helping keep records of their *asusu* (rotating credit association). These early experiences greatly influenced her intellectual and creative life. After graduating from St. Joseph's High School in The Gambia, Khan went on to receive a Bachelor of Arts, two master's degrees, and is currently completing her Ph.D. in African studies at the University of Edinburgh, Scotland. I met Khan for the first time at Timbooktoo Bookstore in 2003, during one of my visits back to The Gambia. By then, she had already received her master's degree from Brandeis University and, as among the new Gambian literati, she was looking for new books to read.

Timbooktoo is the Gambia's foremost literary establishment, something that did not exist when I left the country in the seventies. As a young man in The Gambia, my literary world was limited to the British classics— by William Shakespeare, James Joyce, W. B. Yeats, and George Orwell--at Saint Augustine's High School, and later my writing-apprenticeship encounters with the great late Gambian writer Lenrie Peters. Timbooktoo, however, removed this limitation. The store began as a small, canteen-like bookshop on Pipeline Road, located in the bustling, middle-class neighborhood of Pipeline, near Banjul, the capital city. Before Timbooktoo, the only major bookstore in The Gambia was the Methodist Bookshop, which sold mostly textbooks, stationary, and other educational supplies. Timbooktoo was innovative in that it began stocking books of all kinds—poetry, fiction, memoirs, history, and other reading meant for the general public. It has since grown and moved to a larger building, where it has a coffee shop upstairs, attracts young audiences, and even sponsors occasional readings. It is a haven for readers and connoisseurs of Gambian literature—a place where you can find Gambian writings, by Gambians and on The Gambia, published by international as well as by local publishers, such as Fulladu.

Since our meeting in 2003, Khan and I have been corresponding by email. She has published two poetry collections, *Futa Toro* (2003) and *Juffureh: Kissing You with Hurting Lips,* coauthored with Bamba Khan (2004), and I was particularly struck by the former. The title *Futa Toro* evokes a sense of place and ethnic heritage—the place where the Tukulor or Torodbe ethnic group originated. The Tukulor are culturally sedentary and by pigmentation black, but they share the same traditions and language as the nomadic "red" Fulani. The Tukulor also have a penchant for literacy and learning, and many of West Africa's renowned clerical scholars in Islam are of Tukulor origin. In addition, several prominent West African writers in French and English are also of Tukulor origin, such as Hampate Ba, Cheikh Hamidou Kane, Mariama Ba, Amina Sow Fall, and Amadou Lamine Sall, to name a few.

When I asked Khan why she chose the title *Futa Toro* for her book, she pointed to her syncretic ethnic heritage. Tukulor by ethnic origin, she was raised to pay attention to her family lineage and values as a Khan (sometimes spelled Kane in French) from Futa Toro. She grew up hearing about her ancestors' past exploits, men and women who were notable in the Futa historiography as those, in Khan's own words, "who served God, [and] led the fight for truth and justice for all." Her poetry is also inspired by other roots—a paternal grandmother who belonged to Senegalese Wolof nobility, and a maternal grandmother, who belonged to a Gambian Mandinka clerical family. Together, the Tukulor, Wolof, and Mandinka values of nobility, valor, and love of knowledge greatly influence her worldview and her writing.

In the book's poignant title poem, "Futa Toro," Khan writes:

The shrine of my ancestors
Know when I become

A Fulani born-again
I may speak your tongue
Praise the acrobat decorum
Dance your dances
Sing your songs[1]

This poem expresses one of the anxieties of the contemporary urbanized Tukulor: their loss of linguistic proficiency. Many Tukulor are raised in a predominantly Wolof cultural milieu and are therefore *ipso facto* "Wolofised," neither speaking the Tukulor language nor having a mastery of Tukulor culture and traditions. The poet laments this sense of uprootedness and wishes to be a "Fulani born-again" so that she can master the Fulani rituals of the *reeti* (Fulani violin) and the *piti (*acrobat dancer*)*. But, for the urbanized Tukulor such as the poet, whose engagement with these rituals is only as a periodic observer during weddings or during national celebrations, this generalized nostalgia may be wishful thinking. It may be harking back to an indiscrete cultural identity to which she does not necessarily belong either.

Another poem in the collection, "1981," describes the 1981 Gambian failed coup d'état launched by the adventurist field force paramilitary sergeant, Kukoi Samba Sanyang. The poet was only four years old at the time, but the cataclysmic political events made a lasting impression:

Memorable
Exciting
Awesome
A week of suffering
Hunger, no play
The roads taboo
The guns! Yes the Guns
Kukoi came
Jawara fled
People died, Gambians died
Senegalese came
And died
Jawara brought back
Kukoi escaped

> Bad memory
> I was so young!²

The poem is a sparse recounting of that terrible period of Gambian history, and it expresses both childhood fear and the loss of innocence. Stylistically, it resembles Lenrie Peters's poem, "In the Beginning," with its conversational style, although the topic is grimmer. The child's mind is confused-- "Jawara fled," the poem's persona claims. Of course, in reality, President Jawara, the legitimate leader at the time, did not flee; he was abroad, attending Prince Charles and Lady Diana's wedding, but returned to quell the coup with the Senegalese government's help. But, all the same, perhaps to this young persona, this distinction was not so obvious—indeed, the poet notes with that claim of innocence: "I was so young!"

Similar to Khan, Momodou Sallah too is a noteworthy, emerging Gambian poet. I have never met Sallah, but have spoken to him several times over the phone. He reached out to me from Leicester, England, to write the preface to an anthology of poems by Gambian young adults titled, *A Harvest of Gambian Lines* (2014). I agreed, and we have become "phone and internet" friends since then. Sallah spent his early years in Buckle Street, Banjul, but moved to Old Jeswang, a town located between Banjul, the capital city, and Serrekunda, The Gambia's largest town just eight miles away. Similar to Khan, Sallah, too, is of syncretic ethnic lineage of Tukulor, Wolof, Bambara, and Jola. He describes his early life going to *dara* (a local koranic school), playing indoor soccer in people's half-built houses, hunting hares, and swimming in nearby creeks against the wishes of his parents. His formative years were spent in Pipeline, where he became acting president of the Gambia Student Union and joined the Red Cross, eventually becoming the national youth director of the Gambia Red Cross.

In addition to Sallah's early activism, he continued his education in the United Kingdom, receiving a master's degree in applied social sciences from the University of Leicester, and a doctorate in youth and community development from De Montfort University. Sallah is currently based in the United Kingdom, where he is a professor (Reader) at De Montfort University and is the CEO of Global Hands Publishing, which publishes fiction and nonfiction works by Gambians. Apart from being a promising poet, Sallah has demonstrated, from his early youth, a knack for a variety of entrepreneurial engagement, youth leadership, and community development skills. This passion for community and youth development also comes through in his body of work.

Sallah published a book of poems titled *Innocent Questions* (2012), which deals with a broad spectrum of personal and Pan-African sentiments. One of the collection's most moving poems is "Barca or Berserk." It is a poem about the senseless, perilous journey that many African (and other Third World) youths make to get to Europe. It is a poem tied to what has come to be topically called Europe's migrant problem, a pejorative term reflecting the anti-immigrant feelings among the nationalist segments in the receiving European nations. The poem describes the compulsion that drives many African youths to traverse odds into Europe:

> I must go to Barca or Berserk
> I must go
> I must fly away
> From this jail
> And look for bail
> I drink the Atlantic
> And eat the Sahara
> I swim with sharks
> To escape the economic barks
> I must go to Barca or Berserk[3]

In addition to "push factors"—joblessness at home, hunger, civil conflict, climate change, limited political space, and above all, hopelessness—which the poet describes ominously as "jail," this migration also has "pull factors"—the promise of economic security and a better life. However, the journey to Europe involves risky, unsafe stowaway boats over the shark-filled Atlantic, or crossing the Sahara Desert, playing hide and seek with religious and tribal extremist militias, and transiting through the "failed state" of Libya to get to "Barca" or to "Barcelona." The poem has even more relevance and urgency now as we watch the news of desperate migrants being captured while on transit and sold as slaves in open auctions in Libya.

When I asked Sallah what inspired the "Barca or Berserk" poem, he noted that above all, he wanted to subvert the dominant, erroneous narrative that those making these journeys are "idle and idiotic, aimless, young people." To Sallah, a poet sensitive to the plight of young people, these push factors, which are only becoming worse, must be recognized. The poem's title and refrain is a pun. "I must go to Barca or Berserk" demonstrates the unquenchable compulsion that drives youths to get into Europe. "Barca" may be a reference to Barcelona, or an allusion to any of the migrant-receiving nations of Southern Europe. "Berserk" seems to play with multiple, though similar meanings—whether it means, as in English, "uncontrollable or destructive rage" or "going crazy"; or whether it is a play on the Wolof word, *barsak*, which means "afterlife." Either way, the choices are extreme: the persona in the poem must go to Europe or to craziness; must go to Europe or to death. It is a sinister, youthful calculus.

Bala S. K. Saho is another Gambian poet whose work commands attention. Saho published a book of poems titled *Songs of a Foraging Bird* (2000) and a novella, *The Road to My Village* (1994). He was born and raised in Baddibu Salinkeye, a small town of several hamlets in a region with predominantly Mandinka and Sarahule influences. I first met him in 2016, at the African Studies Association Conference in Washington, DC. He was wearing a suit with no tie, and was bald-headed, tall, and slim. He was affable—not a showman, and a good listener. In our interactions since, the poet described Baddibu Salinkeye as an environment that emphasized family, discipline, and respect. His fascination with history, literature, and culture led him to get bachelor's and master's degrees in history from the Universities of Jyväskylä in Helsinki, Finland. He continued on for another master's degree in African studies from the University of Illinois, Urbana-Champaign, and a Ph.D. in African history from Michigan State University, where he teaches today.

When I interviewed Saho, he expressed his interest in cultural development and in preservation. For years, he worked in the Gambian government's Oral History and Antiquities Division, first working as a transcriber and translator of oral history texts, and later as a curator of the National Museum. By 2010, he was the division's director general. With these administrative experiences under his belt, the poet continues to capture his unique cultural experiences in his poetry.

One of the most poignant lines in his collection, *Songs of a Foraging Bird,* is the poem, "Dedication," written for his mother. In this poem, Saho praises the virtues and hard work of motherhood with grace and gratefulness:

> As long as I live
> I will sing my mother's song
> With her old broom
> That kept our yard forever clean
> And her long hoe
> That kept our stomach full
> Her mortar and pestle
> That grinds our morning porridge
> That bucket of water on her head
> How it kept our minds clean
> Her everyday chorus
> Never mind
> I will paint the world with her smile.[4]

This poem is strung together by three beautiful lines, beginning from "I will sing my mother's song," which expresses the poet's gratefulness to his mother. Then, in the line, "How it kept our minds clean," the poet shows appreciation for his mother's meticulous efforts to fulfill the foundational and biological needs—food, shelter, clothing, and hygiene—which are critical for the development and success of a child's mind. Finally, in the line, "I will paint the world with her smile," the poet demonstrates how his mother's patience and steadfastness, despite her endless toil, is an enduring inspiration for the poet to exercise his creative energies to build a better world. This poem leaves me wanting to see more from this poet.

These modern Gambian poets explore the contemporary challenges facing The Gambia and West Africa. Something immediate and palpable runs in the lines of these poets; they want to speak directly to the public, and communicate what they see and feel not through rinsed eyes and hearts. They do not mind being prosy, like traditional Gambian oral poetry, for the message is it. Unlike the earlier generation of Gambian poets, such as Lenrie Peters, Gabriel Roberts, Swaebou Cornateh, and myself, who wrote poetry, dense with imagery and indirect in their expressions, these poets want to communicate directly with the public by using the language of ordinary speech. The poets show deep sensitivity to their environments, and they pursue culturally relevant themes, which with the new democratic political dispensation, augur well for the future of Gambian poetry.

Notes

1. Mariam Khan, "Futa Toro," in *Futa Toro* (Banjul, Gambia: Sandeng Publishers, 2003), 2.
2. Ibid., 21.
3. Momodou Sallah, "Berca or Berserk," in *Innocent Questions* (Leicester, England: Global Hands Publishing, 2012), 67.
4. Bala K. Saho, "Dedication," in *Song of a Foraging Bird* (2000) (Self published).

CHAPTER 6

TO MY LATE FRIEND DR. LENRIE PETERS: THE GAMBIAN VESSEL EMPTIED OF ITS POETRY

Dr. Lenrie Leopold Wilfred Peters, the founding father of modern Gambian literature and The Gambia's renowned surgeon, poet, and novelist, left us for eternity on May 27, 2009. I will borrow from what W. H. Auden said of W. B. Yeats, "Earth, receive an honored guest,"[1] and The Gambia has lost a great son. Peters departed from us on that fateful May at Hopital Dantec in Dakar, Senegal, after struggling for a while with his health, which resulted in his initial admission to the Kanifing-based Westfield Clinic, one of The Gambia's first private clinics, which he founded with Dr. Samuel J. Palmer. He was then transferred to the national hospital, the Royal Victoria Hospital's Intensive Care Unit, where, because of his inability to arrest his deteriorating condition, he was subsequently rushed to Hopital Dantec, in Senegal. He died of heart failure. He was about seventy-seven years of age.

> Earth, receive an honored guest;
> Lenrie Peters is laid to rest.
> Let the Gambian vessel lie,
> Emptied of its poetry.

Dr. Lenrie Peters is the first son of Pa Lenrie Ernest Ingram Peters and Auntie Kezia Rosemary Peters. Pa Lenrie (a graduate of Sierra Leone's Fourah Bay College, then affiliated with

Durham University, United Kingdom) was a Krio from Sierra Leone and Auntie Kezia Rosemary was a Krio from The Gambia. Lenrie's two older siblings were Bijou Peters-Bidwell (who was married to the late Ernest Bidwell and was trained as a nurse), and Dr. Florence Peters-Mahoney, one of The Gambia's most eminent historians and teachers, who wrote the locally famous national history book, *Stories of The Gambia*. Florence was the first Gambian woman to get a doctorate, and she received it in history at the University of London. Her husband was Dr. John Mahoney Jr., son of Sir John Mahoney, whom the British historian Harry Gailey, described as "one of the leaders of the Bathurst (now Banjul) community in the second quarter of the twentieth century century, the recognized leader of the Mahoney family which counted some of the most educated and influential people in Bathurst."[2] In fact, Hannah Augusta Darling Mahoney, the sister to Dr. John Mahoney Jr., became the first wife of the first prime minister of The Gambia Sir Dawda Kairaba Jawara, and is therefore the first lady of The Gambia. (It should be noted that Sir Dawda had once converted to Chrisitianity and became Sir David K. Jawara and re-converted to Islam in his later years.)

In terms of birth sequence, Lenrie was the first son, but third child in their family. He was followed by a sister, Ruby Peters, who worked for the United Nations Development Programme (UNDP) for many years in an administrative and program management capacity (and who passed away around the same time in 2008), and Dennis Alaba Peters (the last sibling), who had a career as an actor and who died in the United States several years ago. By all accounts, the Peters family were a distinguished lot and have left an indelible mark on the intellectual firmament of The Gambia.

I recalled a day, almost in the late 1990s, during one of my visits to The Gambia being given a lift from Banjul to Serrekunda by M. I. Secka, the ex-auditor general of The Gambia. Secka was a family friend, whom I have had the pleasure of working under during my brief stint out of high school as an audit clerk. On that fortuitous day, while in Secka's car, we spotted Dr. Florence Mahoney walking along Banjul's Independence Drive, wearing a

Mexican-style raffia hat, waving for a taxi. Florence had been Secka's teacher in high school and, as was the respect and courtesy with which teachers were held in those days, Secka stopped to give his old teacher a ride. I had not known Florence personally then, but had been familiar with her enormous contributions to Gambian history. During the ride from Banjul to Serrekunda, near Jeswang or more precisely Sting Corner, where the road formed a fork, Secka diverged toward Bakau/Fajara to drop her old teacher at her house. I kept quiet most of the time, but enjoyed the conversation. What I recalled most memorably was Secka, asking her teacher, who was older, Lenrie or her. Florence remarked forthrightly, "Lenrie is the baby. He is the baby." From my end, in a conversation of elders, the reference to a "baby" can be tricky. Knowing that Lenrie had received his medical degree in 1959, one year after I was born, I could only silently chuckle at the humor of the "baby" reference. Sadly, this "baby," this Lenrie, who was my good friend, has been snatched from us forever by the cruel hands of fate.

Lenrie's family had much hidden, distinguished history behind them. The Peters have direct blood relation with the Maxwells, one of whom was the first African graduate of Oxford University. The Maxwells were, by all accounts, Afro-Victorians and were therefore among Africa's early Westernized elites. Thomas Maxwell, the elder, was a Sierra Leonean of West Indian or Nova Scotian heritage with perhaps Yoruba connections or ancestry, who served as a chaplain to British troops in the British colony of the Gold Coast. Joseph Renner Maxwell, his first son, attended Merton College, Oxford, the first African to do so, and was a law student at Lincoln's Inn, where he graduated in jurisprudence, and following which he served first in the Gold Coast and later rose to be the chief magistrate of The Gambia in 1887.[3]

Joseph, Lenrie's maternal grand uncle, was famous for his book, *The Negro Question*, which, in the prevailing racial despair of those days, recognized the equivalence of the Negro's genius and moral qualities with that of the European, but accepted the aesthetic shortcoming of the Negro and therefore advocated "miscegenation" as a way of improving the Negro's physical aesthetics.[4] Perhaps it is such a predisposition, predicated not on truth or fact but on brainwashing and imbibed psychological shortcomings, which has resulted today in that abominable practice of "skin bleaching" locally known in the Gambia as *hesal*. Joseph was only cleverer than the present-day skin bleachers; he tried to conform to the inadequacies of his times by suggesting to Africans to get rid of their God-given melanin by marrying their lighter-skinned races. Lenrie, of course, was much more enlightened than his Maxwell ancestors were, and he was also a passionate advocate and defender of black and Pan-African causes. He was too enlightened and proud to subscribe to the shortcomings of nineteenth and early twentieth century pigmentation sociobiology for social uplift.

Lenrie's family straddles between Sierra Leone and The Gambia. His family were "Liberated Africans" or *Aku* or *Krio*. The cultural syncretism of "Liberated Africans" made it not that simple to trace tribal lineage to some singular source. Lenrie was aware of this all his life. At the Berlin First Festival of World Cultures held from June 22- to July 15, 1979, the theme was exclusively devoted to African culture. Lenrie admitted at the festival that "I don't belong to a tribe, you see. My family has been detribalized for nearly four generations. So really, I am like Alex Haley. I am looking for my roots."[5] This search for "roots" made Lenrie overwhelmingly preoccupied with the theme of oppression, separation, and return or homecoming in his stylistically perfected and brilliant poetry.

Lenrie's historian-sister, Dr. Florence Mahoney, described the situation of "Liberated Africans," the *Krio*, in a brilliant monograph, "The Liberated Slaves and the Question of Return to Africa":

> The Slave Trade destabilized society and destroyed the mutual respect that existed between Black and White. Above all, it depopulated the region, and impeded development for centuries./The Liberated Slaves who returned to Africa, even before the Abolition of the Slave Trade, were now people of "Two Worlds" with a hybrid culture. They have carried

African beliefs and customs and traditions, and skills…into slavery in the West; they returned with new skills, an English "Creole" language, a new faith—Christianity--, and other customs and traditions, forced upon them./The Liberated Slaves found it difficult to adjust to the indigenous cultures of Africa; and became agents of "Western Civilisation" (introducing Christianity with its churches and schools) wherever they settled. As intermediaries between Black and White peoples, they were distrusted and sometimes hated by both; yet, without them, economic development and modernization would have been further delayed in this region after Abolition. They became the pioneers of Nationalism and Self-government, and laid the foundations of the Independent States of West Africa."[6]

In short, Lenrie's background of coming from the "Liberated African" community, inserted him into an ambivalent position. He was a force of both Western agency and anti-colonial resistance. He was a harbinger for championing Western modernizing values, but also an intellectual force for safeguarding the cultural jewels in the indigenous. Perhaps, it is this unresolved tension which made Lenrie so ambivalent in his poetry, where he champions Africa's greater openness to the world in his poetry collection, *Satellites* (1967) and preservation of indigenous cultural values in his collection, *Katchikali* (1971), The Gambian sacred shrine of crocodiles.

On a personal level, Lenrie was my good friend, whose loss I deeply mourn. Apart from being a world-class medical doctor, he was The Gambia's most renowned writer and indeed the founding father of modern Gambian literature written in English. The Gambia has lost two major literary figures--- Ebou Dibba, a novelist, a few years ago—at a relatively young age, and now that marvelous literary patriarch Lenrie Peters. I got to know Lenrie during my high school years in the early 1970s, and he became both a mentor and a friend. I usually visited him at the Westfield Clinic in Kanifing, where, on the margins of his busy medical practice, he took time off and sat in the yard and reviewed my creative writings and offered advice and encouragement. We became friends ever since. And virtually, every time I visited The Gambia, I visited his house at Cape Point, Bakau, and spent time chatting and getting updated on the goings-on in the country. He will be greatly missed as an inspiring mentor.

Lenrie's writings as a novelist and poet were world-class. His only novel, *The Second Round* (1965) although not so immediately culturally relevant to The Gambia was described by critics, such as Charles Larson, as a "West African gothic," a novel of homecoming, an oeuvre which attempts first to be a work of art and only secondarily "faithful to an African way of life."[7] Yet, apart from The Gambia-born but Sierra Leone-based William Conton's *The African*, Lenrie's novel could very well be the first novel written by a Gambian. Lenrie, however, was best as a poet—and his four poetry collections—*Poems* (Mbari) (1964); *Satellites* (Heinemann) (1967); *Katchikali* (Heinemann) (1971), and the one volume compilation of all of his past and new poetry in *Selected Poetry* (Heinemann) (1981) are among the most intellectual of Africa's contemporary poetry, compared with the poetry of Wole Soyinka. The poems span themes of homecoming (a theme also pursued in his fiction); political satire critical of African dictators—whom Lenrie thought had ruined our continent; celebration of cultural relics like the sacred crocodiles of Katchikali, and personal and universal themes. In almost all of these poems, Peters utilizes occasionally imagery from the natural or medical sciences, but always remains sincere to a Pan-African vision. The Nigeria critic and Lenrie's scholar Romanus Egudu, noted that "Of all modern African poets of English expression, he is the least concerned about his own country and most concerned about the fate of the continent as a whole. He considers himself first an African, and secondly a Gambian."[8] This summed it all: Lenrie was a Pan-Africanist in his thoughts, writings, and conviction. He dreamed, all his life, of a vibrant and revitalized Africa that used its vast resources to develop its citizenry and that stood proud and dignified against the rest of the world. He was a man of substance who shunned empty flamboyance. He will be missed.

What has always impressed me about Lenrie, apart from his obvious literary achievements, was also his entrepreneurial qualities. He was just not only a writer, but a polyvalent, renaissance man. He was one of the first Gambian doctors to go into private practice after a brief stint working for The Gambia government's medical services in places as remote as Bansang Hospital. He was also the owner of a pharmacy; a real estate mogul (owned, e.g., Lenrie House in Banjul, before he sold it); a former broadcaster over the British Broadcasting Corporation (BBC); a chair of the West African Examination Council (WAEC); and the owner of an agribusiness farm in Yundum, Brikama area. One day, during one of my visits to The Gambia, he took me to his farm to see the mangoes he was growing for the export market. He had on his farm a few bore holes and an elaborate irrigation network, and employed local labor. I always used to joke by telling him that "the Gambia needed more Lenrie Peters. And that if we had more like him, we would be a developed country soon." He would smile or chuckle with that characteristic sneaky, bellylaugh, as he was suppressing a rich African humanity under some Anglo-Saxon reserve.

Lenrie spoke perfect Cambridge University English; in fact, it was rare to find an African or, for that matter, British with an English more polished. I used to say to myself that, if one were to hear Lenrie speaking behind a wall without seeing him in person, one would think it was the voice of a high-class English gentleman. His voice was distinctive and authoritative, and he read his poetry with a melodic, Anglo-Saxon cadence. In fact, given the privileged, if not elevated status, with which the English language was held in the former colonies, The Gambians found Lenrie's English amusing, if not downright intimidating. Locally, some people used to say in Wolof, *Lenrie kaing, toubab la,* a derogatory reference that "Lenrie was a white man" because he spoke perfect Cambridge English and kept himself aloof from local, idle chitchat and social circles. For me this accusation was mere trivia, for if one truly knew Lenrie, it was never the British sound of his accent that mattered, but his deep African humanity and commitment to African culture.

Lenrie knew both of my parents and was also my parents' doctor, especially when they needed critical surgeries. He had performed surgery on both of my parents on a few occasions. The last one was on my father, who, at age ninety-three, had fallen and suffered a hip fracture. Lenrie did the surgery and, for a while, my father did well; but later, not atypical of folks of his age, he developed blood clots, his condition worsened, and he succumbed to eternity. I was still in the United States, but I was told that Lenrie would come every day to our house to check on my father's progress. But my father was battling overwhelming odds; age was not in his favor, and he finally succumbed to the odds. What always struck me about Lenrie was his self-effacing kindness. He was not given to self-promotion common among local elites in the repertoire of local praise singers. In much of the medical services he provided to my parents, he would always ask for less or no fees, but my parents, being self-responsible and independent characters, would always insist on paying in full, and finally and reluctantly Lenrie would accept payment. However, that gesture of willingness to help out at all cost is the real mark of this great man.

Some of my recollections of Lenrie were letters he wrote to me in longhand, always encouraging me while I was a student, like a paternal big brother. The letters were a testament to our long and enduring friendship. One of the earliest letters I could find from him was dated July 22, 1982. It was one of the longer letters I have received from him and it was during my last year as an undergraduate student at Berea College in Kentucky. We had met, a few months earlier, at an African Literature Association (ALA) Conference held at the Claremont Colleges in California. The Claremont ALA was one of the best attended, and featured several major African writers, such as the late Mongo Beti of Cameroon; the late Florent Nwapa ---and Buchi Emecheta of Nigeria; Aminata Sow Fall of Senegal; the late Dennis Brutus, Cecile Abrahams (brother to Peter Abrahams), and Fatima Dike of South Africa; George Lamming, Maryse Conde, and Paule Marshall from the Caribbean; Miriam Were of Kenya; Peter Nazareth of Uganda; Kofi Anyidoho from Ghana; and many more. Lenrie, Professor Mbye Cham of Howard University, and I were the only representatives who were Gambian, and Lenrie was the only one who flew from The Gambia. Lenrie had not known about Cham and asked me whether he was Senegalese, which I quickly corrected. In attendance were also all the usual suspect veteran critics and professors attending the Claremont ALA Conference: Bernth Lindfors; the late Robert M. Wren; Emile Snyder; Stephen Arnold; Kenneth Harrow; Aliko Songolo; Jonathan Peters; Onyekan Owomoyela; Chikwenye Okonjo Ogunyemi; Marie Umeh; Donald Burness; Donald and Margaret Herdeck (publishers of Three Continents Press); Lee Nichols from the BBC; and Professor Daniel Kunene.

Following the Claremont event, Lenrie wrote to me the following letter:

> Dear Tijan, Your letter arrived a few days ago and I felt I must just reply before I leave for Europe in a few days; so do forgive shortcomings. I am going to Vienna and Saltzburg. /Some weeks ago, I met your rather inconsolable father outside the Post Office (*in Banjul, Gambia's capital city*, italics mine), largely on your mother's behalf, because they had not heard from you. I consoled them with the probability of exams, etc. A week later, he was smiling again and told me of your successes. /The only lone joy is self-fulfillment and I am proud that you're taking all that comes your way and turning silver into gold. I can only say as Henry James said to a talented young person, "You have fashioned yourself a magic carpet; stand on it!" I endorse the precious letter, which you so kindly sent me. /No, I decided not to attend the ALA this year and read comments in West Africa magazine. I have had reservations about the trends within. It is becoming too much of a political forum for some uses, and also too much of a high school performance. I think the format ought to be looked again. After my very first visit, I felt certain that to give it meaning, even occasional meetings should be held on African soil. The suggestion didn't go down well when I made it. And the attitude was typical, "Alright! Find the money!" /I offered a report to Hugh Quashie with all downtrodden and acquiescing authors in mind. Reviewing and criticism use to

be an art form once, when the critic expanded and contributed to the creative work. Alas, cutting corners as we have to do in almost every aspect of African life, anybody with a few letters attached consider themselves competent to lash into critical print. I feel also that editors have a responsibility towards authors as to whom they invite to review their work and also as to whether acceptance of such reviews are automatic. /We have had a busy year setting up a museum at the Old British Council Library building—opposite Sam Jack Terrace. This will soon be completed and opened. Then after 18 months closure of the Gambia College, we're opening in October at the new campus in Brikama. We have an experienced Ghanaian to help set it up for 2 years with a view to a Gambian taking over at that time. There is a dearth of commitment or sense of vocation to the community. Everybody is plucking at the next big job; so that there is little continuity. Reminds me of the *weyus* (*i.e., street ruffians, italics mine*) throwing stones at the mangoes and scrambling after the fallen fruit. Here we have a new college, a new principal, and a new permanent secretary. It means that one is forever starting again from the beginning. /I can't talk about poetry this time, except to say that I like and admire your work. / Keep the flag flying. / Sincerely, Lenrie P.

The last letter I could find from Lenrie was dated July 11, 1993, and was on a West African Examinations Council (WAEC) letterhead with a Westfield Clinic address and had Lenrie as the chair of WAEC. Lenrie's long association with WAEC demonstrated his devoted commitment to the development of young minds in West Africa. I had just returned to the United States after a visit to The Gambia. His letter read:

Dear Tijan, That you came and went without my spending another hour with you has grieved me. Frankly, that was a sad week for me. An estate agent, whom I had asked to handle my property, had swindled me of 65,000 Dalasis. He is going to be prosecuted, if he doesn't pay up. There were also problems in the farm. / Not being a reviewer, I did not feel obliged to gobble up "Dreams of Dusty Roads" (i.e., *Tijan's book of poems,* italics mine). Now, I've been through sipping it like good wine, with great pleasure. I can hear your own authentic voice in (the poem), say, "Shadows of Banjul" and so many other gems. /But how does one escape the... with ideas? Beyond, it seems to me, lies the pure distillation of experience, or whatever you call it. / I enjoyed your articles in the *Observer*--- a refreshing change from the everyday. Though we should not complain. The *Observer* has introduced a new trend and mental discipline in Banjul Society. What one never missed before has taken a central place in the life of the community. At last, one no longer have to learn of the local news through the BBC. Best wishes to your wife and self, Sincerely, Lenrie.

In another letter, he wrote me from Dakar on May 2, 1987, on a Novotel letterhead, it read:

My dear Tijan, I am in Dakar and brought your letter and publications with me in the hope of having the time to write you a long letter. This is the 27th Annual Meeting of the West African College of Surgeons, and our Senegalese brothers are giving us a taste of their usual arrogance and indifference. The meetings are held in FIDAC, near the Airport (i.e., Leopold Sedar Senghor Airport) where the Social Fairs take place. No cars are provided, so that when we get there in the morning, we have to stay until evening, whether we are participating or not. / Thank you very much for your good works, even more for letting me share your successes in literature. I will try to write a long letter another time; but for now--- well done and keep it going. / Best wishes, Sincerely, Lenrie P.

Well, friend, we will try to keep "it" going, but I am not sure whether it will ever be the same without you. You meant so much to us, and your departure has taken so much from us. In my view, Lenrie was one of The Gambia's greatest personalities. In our short lives, the mark of greatness is not in how much pain and suffering we impose on humanity, but in how much good deeds and great thoughts we leave behind to advance the welfare of our human family. Undoubtedly, Lenrie has left us jewels on all of these fronts. He was hardworking, creative, and committed. He spent his entire life in private medical practice, serving the enormous medical needs of The Gambian population. For his times, Lenrie was highly educated, but, unlike us the selfish ones abroad, he did not choose an easier and more lucrative life by working abroad; instead, he chose to spend his entire working life serving the people of The Gambia. He was a true patriot, who truly deserves our honor. Lenrie was one of those few and necessary Gambian men who will be forever remembered for putting The Gambia on the world's literary map. May his great soul, which has touched me personally and touched many around the world, rest in peace.

Notes

1   Helen Gardner, ed, *The New Oxford Book of English Verse* (Oxford: Oxford University Press, 1990): 920.
2   Hary Gailey, *Historical Dictionary of The Gambia* (New Jersey: The Scarecrow Press, 1975), 89.
3   Pamela Roberts, *Black Oxford: The Untold Stories of Oxford University's Black Scholars* (Oxford: Signal Books, 2013), 82.
4   Ibid., 83.
5   Al Imfeld, *Portraits of African Writers: Lenrie Peters, Horizons 1979 First Festival of World Culture* (Bonn: Deutsche Welle, 1979), 3.
6   Florence Mahoney, *The Liberated Slaves and The Question of The Return to Africa: From the Slave Trade to the Challenge of Development* (Kanifing, The Gambia: Book Production and Material Resources Unit, 2001), 1.
7   Charles Larson, *The Emergence of African Fiction* (Bloomington: Indiana University Press, 1972), 227-41.
8   Romanus Egudu, *Four West African Poets* (New York: Nok, 1977).

CHAPTER 7

PHILLIS WHEATLEY: A BRIEF SURVEY OF THE LIFE AND WORKS OF A GAMBIAN SLAVE-POET IN NEW ENGLAND AMERICA

The thought of a poet, black and female, in eighteenth-century America triggers images of eccentric white, male chauvinists brandishing their protest-placards, self-assured against the possible. But this thought was realized in the person of the able and seemingly unsettling literary career of Phillis Wheatley. It is important here that we examine her life and her works in the context of the social milieu that she operated.

Scholarly consensus trace Phillis's place of birth to the general region of Senegambia. In her own poetic works, she mentioned The Gambia as her place of origin and fondly made nostalgic references to it as the landscape where her "soul returns." Phillis is generally believed to have been born in 1753, but was unfortunately taken away as a slave to New England, America, in 1761. She was sold, as was the custom, to Mr. and Mrs. John Wheatley, under whose custody she found much favor because of her natural talents and self-invigorating wit. Because of her self-assured disposition, her masters became so increasingly impressed by her, that they made her a share-owning member of the family's assets.[1]

The close relation which Phillis had with her masters reflected not only the residual humanity of the power wielders, but also showed the African capacity to engage wit (as the proverbial hare against the hyena) to survive the heavy-handed brawl of the scepter-wielders. Phillis's genius, despite the unfavorable odds and temperament of the period, is best described by her own master, John Wheatley, in that tellingly revealing introduction to her book, *Poems on Various Subjects, Religious and Moral* (1773):

> Phillis was brought from Africa to America,
> in the Year 1761, between seven and eight
> Years of Age. Without any Assistance from
> School Education, and by only what she was
> taught in the Family, she, in sixteen Months
> Time from her Arrival, attained the English
> Language, to which she was an utter Stranger
> before, to such a degree, as to read any, the
> most difficult Parts of the Sacred Writings, to
> great Astonishment of all who heard her.
> As to her Writing, her own Curiosity led her
> to it; and this she learnt in so short a Time,
> that in the Year 1765, she wrote a Letter to the
> Rev. Mr. Occom, the Indian Minister, while in
> England.
> She has a great Inclination to learn the Latin
> Tongue, and has made some Progress in it. This
> Relation is given by her Master who bought her, and
> with whom she now lives.[2]

This introduction to Phillis's book was dated November 14, 1772, and it is as much a laudatory statement of the poet's personal self-drive as it is a testimony of the violation of the prejudged expectations that her masters had of her. The mention that the poet performed intellectual feats to the "great astonishment of all who heard her," indeed suggests that the poet's genius surpassed the standards set for her and, indeed, hinged on the extraordinary.

Phillis's genius is not altogether divorced from her territory of origin. The region of Senegambia has always been a fertile ground for bards and minstrels, storytellers and griots, saints, and sages. So it is not entirely surprising that Phillis, a product of that rich heritage, who, though may have suffered early transplantation away from the source, nonetheless retained in those inner recesses of her subconscious, those early childhood experiences, rites, and rituals, which survived as flashback images and symbols, mnemonic devices for the actualization of her artistic genius.

In assessing her as a poet and as a racial symbol, it is important to note that Phillis rides on the reputation-horse of being one of the first, if not the first, black American poet. But this "founding mother" role has not assured her an unblemished reputation in critical appraisals of her oeuvres. She has both been lauded and reprimanded in her works, which perhaps is healthy since mixed reactions often imply artistic balance and the mysterious complexity of an individual artist's mind. Phillis has been condemned (and perhaps unfairly) for the "piety in her art"; for being soft on slavery; for showing minimal interest in "her race and the land of her origin; for being "abstract, polite, restrained"; for being "negative, bloodless," and possessing and "unracial quality"; and for being, in short, "unequipped for abolitionism."[3] These criticisms, however, are largely contemporary, giving little allowance to the prevailing circumstances of cultural and personal oppression that she operated under. These criticisms fly in the face of Phillis's symbolic significance in the positive refutation of the false myths about the "congenital inferiority of the Negro" which were so passionately held and defended by single-minded advocates of New World slavery.

It should be noted that, around this time, the nature of the "Negro"--his cerebral and cognitive capacity--was the subject of serious speculation. Definition of the "Negro" outside the European ethnocentric (or narrow) circle of humanity was pursued with the missionary zeal of a misguided cult, leading to various pseudoscientific theories which provided the scaffold for the continued sustenance of inhumane New World slavery. Henry Louis Gates Jr.'s work on Phillis detailed this relation between the nature of the Negro's "racial self," and Phillis's symbolic significance. In a carefully reasoned argument, Gates notes:

> Impassioned and detailed biblical exegesis, which for two and half centuries had tried to fit the rapidly proliferating kinds of persons into an order ordained by God; the wildly speculative natural philosophy which clung, rather perilously to the

metaphor of the chain; the bemused arrangements, by cranial capacity, of the "progressively" larger skulls of ape and man; the creative and imaginative descriptions of black humanity repeated with such enthusiasm by the European discoveries of Africa; and a received metaphorical system which had consistently made the color black analogous with the shade of evil—all these complex matters lay buried beneath the debate over the natural rights of the African and his or her fitness for enslavement. As surely as the temporalization of the chain of being had led eventually to its demise as a valid construct by which philosophy could account for the order of things, so too had the American colonists' fundamental belief in a quantity they could call "the rights of man" led them to declare a belief in the determining power of environment on the reshaping of a human nature which had to be, by definition, "everywhere the same."[4]

This seemingly obvious conclusion about the equivalence of humanity across the racial spectrum and the preponderance of environmental factors in "reshaping" human nature was not so apparent during Phillis's lifetime. Comforting appeals to the Bible to rationalize European instincts only fortified European prejudices. So it is "ironic that Phillis Wheatley, who so painstakingly located her poetry within a larger and peculiarly Puritan tradition of Christian piety, would have her slim volume of verse utilized as prima facie evidence in a fundamentally secular debate over the rights of man."[5] Phillis's symbolic significance was that she was both black and female--and also a Christian poet. In terms of the European temperament of her times, the first two characteristics ipso facto automatically set her at a disadvantage. But Phillis's acumen outweighed the asinine tendencies of her detractors; and her genius, therefore, served as the living proof of the "mental and aesthetic capacity of the African slave," and hence the necessity for slavery-abolition.[6]

It is a peculiar, though not atypical, feature of Phillis's poetic career that when her works were about to be published, some race-conscious skeptics raised doubts about whether a "Negro Girl" of her disadvantage could come up with such mastery of language and artistic prowess which, until then, was the privileged undertaking of exalted souls. Her publisher, entirely convinced that Phillis wrote the poems, nonetheless secured supporting signatures from some of the most honorable gentlemen of Boston to assure the world that the poems were indeed the imaginative products of a black soul. The attestation read:

> As it has been repeatedly suggested to the Publisher, by Persons, who have seen the Manuscript, that Numbers would be ready to suspect they were not really the Writings of PHILLIS, he has procured the following attestation, from the most respectable Characters in Boston, that none might have the least Ground for disputing their Original.
> WE whose Names are under-written, do assure the
> World, that the POEMS specified in the following Page, were (as verily believe) written by Phillis, a young Negro Girl, who was but a few Years since, brought an uncultivated Barbarian from Africa, and has ever since been, and now is, under the Disadvantage of serving as a Slave in a Family in this Town. She has been examined by some of the best Judges, and is thought qualified to write them.[7]

Among those who signed this attestation to Phillis's competence were the governor, Thomas Hutchinson, and the lieutenant governor, Andrew Oliver. That such eminent personalities would take particular interest in the work of the poet shows the centrality of her role in the larger existential debate about the capability of the African. There is in the attestation some element of condescending flatulence which has no basis in the provable. The god-complex which fed the ambition of the signers, which gave them the preemptive posture to render the verdict of "uncultivated Barbarian" on another human, which made them bloated with a self-exaltation pursued at the expense of diminishing the humanity of the other-- all these stood in stark contrast to the strategic and principled uniqueness of Phillis in dispelling the received racial fog from the minds of the complacent.

It is a curious aspect of the America of Phillis's times that doubts were raised about an "uncultivated Barbarian's" ability to write high-minded poetry.⁸ Although it is self-servingly polemical (and may indeed not be entirely helpful) to juxtapose one's ancestors against another's in the interminable quest for who had superior ancestry, the temptation could not be resisted but to state that the European ancestry of white Americans was not, after all, the most "cultivated," as described succinctly by the French Champollion whose writings we access through the scholarly works of the late African scholar, Cheikh Anta Diop. Champollion captures some revealing facts about the ancestors of Europeans in what is considered the "oldest ethnological document available" this document "concerns bas-reliefs on the tomb of Sesostris I, also visited by Rienzi. These date back to the sixteenth century BC (Eighteenth Dynasty) and represent the races of man known to the Egyptians."⁹ After a description that the "Egyptians and Africans (were) represented in the same way," Champollion states this about the European:

> Finally, the last one is what we call flesh-colored, a white skin of the most delicate shade, a nose straight or slightly arched, blue eyes, blond or reddish beard, tall stature and very slender, clad in a hairy ox-skin, a veritable savage tattooed on various parts of his body; he is called Tamhou.¹⁰

"Tamhou," the archetype-European ancestor, is referred here by a European scholar as "veritable savage." To the extent that Europeans, from their earlier state of "veritable savagery," were able to produce a William Shakespeare and a Charles Baudelaire, there appears to me little reason why doubts were raised about Africa's ability to produce a Phillis Wheatley and, for that matter, an Aleksandr Pushkin.

The "view from here" (to borrow a phrase popularized by the late African-American writer Jimmy Baldwin) is that Phillis, apart from being a rara avis, was a symbolic embodiment of a positive myth--a personal myth that stood in contradistinction (and quite ably provided a counterexample) to that self-serving thesis quite ceremoniously popularized by Europeans which often treated those outside of European humanity as quiescent; which saw their humanity as suspect; which saw the indigenous peoples of Africa,

Asia, Australia, and America as inferior specimens of the human genus; which created a lamentable hierarchical vocabulary, enriched by racist metaphors and intimidating clichés, so pronounced as to lend support to the pseudomythical "white man's burden" and which candidly expected no positive novelty from Africans and from other non-Europeans; and which therefore provided the egoistic justification for Europeans' condescending treatment of those that the Nigerian critic Chinweizu aptly described as the "rest of us."[11]

In order to appreciate more fully Phillis's symbolic significance, we now turn briefly to her poetic works and then revert to her life's travails and personal struggles in the quest for reducing enormous odds into a ladder for a humane vision. Phillis's poetry is rich in Biblical references and in African allusions which reveals the degree to which her poetic imagination has been shaped by her experiences in both worlds. In one of her poems, "Philis's Reply to the Answer," she specifically made references to her place of origin, combining that unrelenting power to employ memory in the service of art to the extent of even exaggeration or sentimental throwback into a bygone world. The poem goes:

> Charm'd with thy painting, how my bosom burns!
> And pleasing Gambia on my soul returns,
> With native grace in spring's luxuriant reign,
> Smiles the gay mead, and Eden blooms again,
> The various bower, the tuneful flowing stream,
> The soft retreats, the lovers golden dream,
> Her soil spontaneous, yields exhaustless stores;
> For phoebus revels on her verdant shores.[12]

If the "heaven" that Phillis paints here was truly The Gambia she was taken away from, then that world cannot simultaneously be a "heaven" and a "barbaric world" to warrant her being an "uncultivated barbarian." Of course, Phillis was young when she was uprooted from The Gambia, and the romanticization of The Gambia--the allusion to a world of pristine beauty, replete with natural bounties, a heaven, and a Garden of Eden before the Fall-- all these point to her capacity as a poet to indulge in regenerative nostalgia, to let that maturing mind loose on an imagined landscape, to retrieve a "lost world" surviving in the form of faint childhood memories; to, in short, dream about the past. But this capacity to dream about the past could as much be informed by truths as by falsehoods, facts as by fiction. To what extent can we willingly trust childhood recollections rendered through a fictive medium as truth goes beyond our capacity here to provide an easy answer. All we can honestly say is that Phillis in the poem felt an elevated respect for her place of origin and demonstrated a psychic attachment to it which was as much informed by an involuntary alienation as by a nostalgic plunge to transcend the strictures imposed by space and time.

One of the peculiar features of Phillis's poetry, as demonstrated in the aforementioned poem, is the liberal use of ornamental imagery. Her poetics seemed generally to have been influenced by those of Alexander Pope and other neoclassicals. Gates gives us a succinct recapitulation of the features which deck the interiority of Phillis's poetics.

> Imitating Pope in rhythm and meter, Wheatley wrote in decasyllabic lines of closed heroic couplets. There is much use of invocation, hyperbole, and inflated ornamentation, and overemphasis of personification, all of which characterize neoclassical poetry.[13]

One should also add that a persistent feature of Phillis's poetry, which perhaps is characteristic of neoclassical poetry in general, is the seeming attempt at an artistry which displays (rather than embodies) erudition. Deliberate references to Biblical or Greek images were employed to perhaps show "learnedness." This is perhaps understandable for an artist who stood on a defensive stage; who had something to prove; and who knew that any attempt at simplicity or at ordinariness risked being misunderstood not only for a lack of "ability," but also for a lack of profundity.

So, Phillis's poetry bristled with Greek references such as "Apollo," "Aesculapius," "Olympus," "Thebans," "Phrygian," and Biblical references such as "Cain," "David," "Goliath," "Israel,"

"Jacob," "Beelzebub," "Jesus," and "Eliab." In a continuation of the poem just cited, the poet continued to paint The Gambian landscape with her poetic brush in the same dreamy tone:

> Whose flowery births, a fragrant train appear,
> And crown the youth throughout the smiling year,
> There, as in Britain's favor'd isle, behold
> The bending harvest ripen into gold!
> Just as thy views of Afric's blissful plain....[14]

These lines showed that Phillis had pleasant memories of The Gambia and this is best exemplified in the reference to "Afric's blissful plain." But was Africa's supposedly "blissful plain" also not the territory of "pain" from which she was cruelly snatched? It is clear that the memories are evoked with a romanticized flair, dragged into the realm of comparative reference, as in the reference to "Britain's favor'd isle," perhaps a literary symbol representing "England."

It is interesting to note that in 1773, Phillis's literary fortunes peaked. She visited England under the patronage of the elites of London's society. Upon her return to Boston, Massachusetts, she was given a hero's welcome, and hailed as the "extraordinary Poetical Genius."[15] Such festive fanfare did not only stop with accolades, but also entailed residual gains translated into greater freedom.

Phillis, as the accomplished poetic genius who jerked white expectations about the nature of the "Negro" to humble and realistic proportions, was never a comfortable muse resting on her laurels. A sense of extended sympathy with the general condition of her race pervaded her freedom crusades and occupied her literary imagination. She challenged prevailing "doxas" or "unexamined beliefs" which characterized the received wisdom of genteel, New England white society, and revealed the contradictions apparent in the overt and enthusiastic manifestations of American white celebration of her talent and the plain denial of natural rights to the Negro.

Sometimes Phillis's position was curiously apologetic and she appeared self-catapulted on to the mission of being her race's mouthpiece:

> 'Twas mercy brought me from my Pagan land,
> Taught my benighted soul to understand
> That there's a God, that there's a Savior too:
> Once I redemption neither sought nor knew,
> Some view our sable race with scornful eye,
> "Their Color is a diabolic die."
> Remember, Christians, Negroes, Black as Cain,
> May be refin'd, and join th'Angelic train.[16]

This poem titled, "On Being Brought from Africa to America," written by fourteen- year-old Phillis and published in 1768, received celebrated reception from the British press. The poem has been explained by a critic as a case for the "mutability of blackness,"[17] but it is that and more. It is a poem, of course, which acknowledges the open possibilities for salvation of the "Negro," but it is also a poem which implicitly suggests the identical humanity of all races. As "pagan Europe" went through a spiritual transformation to abandon heathen ways for the light of Christ, so was "pagan Africa" capable of a similar Christian redemption. There is, however, a condescending tone in the poem which may appear as self-flagellation before our modern eyes-- especially the reference to "Cain" and to "sable race." But one can speculate that this may have been a reflection of a personal inadequacy on the part of a young girl overwhelmed by an environment in which very little of the surrounding values and beliefs led to self-affirmation.

It is interesting to compare this early apologetic self-apprehension with that of the later more mature Phillis who, through a geriatric burst of thunderbolt energy, revealed the hypocrisies of white racial duplicity-- or more succinctly, white double standards. In her letter of February 11, 1774, published in the *Connecticut Gazette* and reprinted in four Boston papers, and also in newspapers in New Haven, Newport, Providence, and Salem, Phillis presented a passionate argument before the Reverend

Samson Occom about the Negro's and, for that matter, the human's propensity to embrace freedom.[18] The letter read:

> The following is an extract of a Letter from Phillis, a Negro Girl of Mr Wheatley's, in Boston, to the Rev. Samson Occom, which we are desired to insert as a Specimen of her Ingenuity. It is dated 11th (Feb.,) 1774.
>
> Rev'd and honor'd Sir,
>
> "I HAVE this Day received your obliging kind Epistle, and am greatly satisfied with your Reasons Respecting the Negroes, and think highly reasonable what you offer in Vindication of their natural Rights:
> Those that invade them cannot be insensible that the divine Light is chasing away the thick Darkness which broods over the Land of Africa; and the Chaos which has reigned so long, is converting into beautiful Order, and reveals more clearly the glorious Dispensation of civil and religious Liberty, which are so inseparably united, that there is little or no Enjoyment of one without the other: Otherwise, perhaps, the Israelites had been less solicitous for their Freedom from Egyptian Slavery; I don't say they would have been contented without it, by no Means, for in every human Breast, God has implanted a Principle, which we call Love of Freedom; it is impatient of Oppression, and pants for deliverance; and by the Leave of our modern Egyptians I will assert, that the same principle lives in us. God grant Deliverance in his own Way and Time, and get him honour upon all those whose Avarice impels them to countenance and help forward the Calamities of their fellow Creatures.
> This I desire not for their Hurt, but to convince them of the strange Absurdity of their Conduct whose Words and Actions are so diametrically opposite. How well the cry for Liberty, and the reverse Disposition for the exercise of oppressive Power over others agree, --I humbly think it does not require the Penetration of a Philosopher to determine.[19]

This letter revealed Phillis's three aspects: one is the Biblical influences on her temper as exemplified in the utilization of the Hebrew paradigm of liberation into the Promised Land from

Egyptian slavery. The second aspect is the influence of white American and European ideas about Africa on her imagination. The final aspect is a more assertive and self-thinking Phillis who domesticated existing philosophical thought to reveal the absurdity and contradictions of white American behavior toward the Negro. To Phillis, the Principle of Freedom is a natural, inalienable right. It was indeed contradictory that white American colonists around this time were crying for liberation and independence from the "Old World" tyranny (which was the very basis for their flight away from Europe) and yet still then engaging in the most heinous crimes of treating the Negro as a chattel slave. Freedom, indeed, for white Americans was a self-circumscribed good, self-appropriated for their race and denied to others (Negroes and Native Americans or "Indians").

Switching back to her poetry, Phillis valued not only the principle of freedom, but also other virtues. In her poem, "On Virtue," she sings:

> O Thou bright jewel in my aim I strive
> To comprehend thee. Thine own words declare
> Wisdom is higher than a fool can reach.
> I cease to wonder, and no more attempt
> Thine height t'explore, or fathom thy profound.
> But, O my soul, sink not into despair,
> Virtue is near thee, and with gentle hand
> Would now embrace thee, hovers o'er thine head.[20]

Piety in her work becomes apparent as she made references to the "soul," and to "virtue" that becomes a form of "grace," a gift of God, which is effortlessly near the human condition and which is attainable through negation of despair-- through the exaltation of hope.

To surmise, the poetry and life of Phillis Wheatley reveals a certain redemptive piety which shows that she was deeply immersed in Biblical teachings. Her poetry, however, has been read and criticized often in non-literary terms which may be symbolic of her larger role as the embodiment of a positive, personal myth: the African woman as a full human being with all of the self-authenticating qualities and frailties found among other races of human beings. As Louis Gates, succinctly notes:

> Although viewers seem to have found much in her work that is genuinely "poetic," her verse, criticized rarely, seems to have been read primarily in nonliterary terms and for other than literary purposes.[21]

And this is understandable for Phillis was more than just a poet embarked on "art for art's sake"—indeed, she would probably have received much less attention today if her art was not a reflection of the human condition she was confronted with.

Phillis's genius and contributions must continue to be remembered as the diasporic assertion of a woman-- black and Christian-- who, though faced with seemingly insurmountable odds, rose to the challenge to assert, through her unique gifts, the equal humanity of the African vis-à-vis the European. This, of course, was a novel and brave claim during her time, for the very rationale of slavery embodied the denial of this equivalence. Phillis died in 1784--and indeed this reflected the curtailment of an important Senegambian flame burning through the labyrinths of supposedly genteel New England America. There are two tragic events which may have hastened her end: her turbulent marriage to John Peters, a black man, on April 1, 1778, and the deaths of her master and mistress, Mr. and Mrs. John and Sussana Wheatley in March 1778 and 1774, respectively, which were shortly followed by declines in her fortunes.[22] Phillis's death symbolized the end of an exemplary African woman who, albeit "snatch'd from Afric's fancy'd happy seat" at infancy, nonetheless assumed the posture of a moral crusader who fought against the superstructural rationalizations for racial oppression.

Notes

1   Johnson Morris et al., *From Freedom to Freedom: African Roots in American Soil* (New York: Random House, 1977), 73.

2. Phillis Wheatley, *Poems on Various Subjects, Religious and Moral* (Philadelphia: Joseph Crukshank, 1786), vii.
3. Muktar Ali Isani, "'Gambia on My Soul': Africa and the African in the Writings of Phillis Wheatley," *Melus*, 6 (Spring 1979), 64.
4. Henry Louis Gates Jr., *Figures in Black: Words, Signs, and the "Racial" Self* (New York: Oxford University Press, 1987), 72.
5. Ibid.
6. Ibid., 74.
7. Wheatley, *Poems on Various Subjects, Religious and Moral*, 8.
8. H. L. Gates Jr. notes in a preface to the *The Collected Works of Phillis Wheatley* (1988) edited by John Shields that "This curious anecdote, surely one of the oddest oral examinations on record, is only a tiny part of a larger, and even more curious, episode in the Enlightenment. Since the beginning of the sixteenth century, Europeans had wondered aloud whether or not the African "species of men," as they they were commonly called, could ever create formal literature, could ever master "the arts and sciences." If they could, the argument ran, then the African variety of humanity was fundamentally related to the European variety. If not, then it seemed clear that the African was destined by nature to be a slave. This was the burden shouldered by Phillis Wheatley when she successfully defended herself and the authorship of her book against counterclaims and doubts. /Indeed, with her successful defense, Wheatley launched two traditions at once—the black American literary tradition and the black woman literary tradition."
9. Cheikh Anta Diop, *The African Origin of Civilization—Myth or Reality* (West Port: Lawrence Hill,1974), 46; see also Maurice Delafosse, *Negroes of Africa* (Washington, DC: The Associated Publishers, 1931), 20-21.
10. Ibid. 47.
11. Chinweizu, *The West and the Rest of Us* (Lagos, Nigeria: Pero Press, 1987).
12. Isani, "Gambia on My Soul," 69.
13. Gates, *Figures in Black*,73.
14. Isani, "Gambia on My Soul," 67.
15. Ibid., 66-68
16. Wheatley, *Poems on Various Subjects Religious or Moral*, 11.
17. Gates, *Figures in Black*, 73.
18. Isani, "Gambia on My Soul," p. 67.
19. Ibid., 67-68.
20. Wheatley, *Poems on Various Subjects Religious or Moral*,11.
21. Gates, *Figures in Black*, 73.
22. Isani, "Gambia on My Soul," 66-70.

CHAPTER 8

HARLEM RENAISSANCE: THOUGHTS ON THE MOVEMENT AND ON ITS POETRY

No literary movement in the history of the African-American compares favorably with the Harlem Renaissance in terms of its rich awareness of Africa, artistic variety, concentration of high-caliber talent, and single-minded commitment to freedom. Poetry was a popular art form of the Movement as well as other literary genres—short and long fiction, and plays. Jazz, spirituals/gospels, blues, and dancing were also part of the Movement. This essay looks at the poetry of the Movement. It examines the factors which gave birth to it, Harlem's unique centrality to it, and the Renaissance's cultural contribution to American civilization particularly in its accomplished artistry (concentrating here primarily on its poetry).

As a cultural nationalist movement, the Harlem Renaissance concentrated on the theme of "the New Negro"—who was born-again but with an informed pride about his culture and history. Black scholars, artists, common people, and their white patrons merged together in Harlem to reexamine history in a new light-- not as it was historically distorted to perpetuate the self-serving and all-too-convenient myth of white supremacy—but as a fair reexamination and re-interpretation and celebration of lived truths-- the truths of the "Negro" past, recalibrated and revalued with its glorious achievements. The Movement, in short, tried to rescue the

"Negro" from the distortions and scorn for which white oppression had made of the Negro's glorious ancestry and history.

Numerous factors combined to produce the Harlem Renaissance--the most important being an honest reevaluation of the weighty legacy of slavery. After abolition, the conditions of blacks in the American South turned increasingly hopeless. The "Negro" was deprived of his civil rights, forced into "separate but equal" schools, transportation, hotels, restaurants, and other public facilities, and was subjected to servitude.[1] Increasingly more oppressive conditions resulted in the Negro exodus from the rural South to the urban North--especially to Harlem-- where the promise lay of better wages and more tolerable working conditions and social relations with white counterparts prevailed. Harlem, thus, was the mecca of black opportunity[2]-- the place of black awareness of their struggle as not only a national one, but one with global implications. The American "Negro" was to come in contact with blacks from the Caribbean and from Africa, and to share the universal experiences of the peoples of his race.[3]

Another factor which gave rise to the Renaissance was the radical inspiration which came from a coterie of black intellectuals, such as the Jamaican Marcus Aurelius Garvey, the African-American Booker T. Washington, and W.E.B. Du Bois. Garvey's ideas and speeches influenced thoughts of the Renaissance writers, especially his popular philosophy of "African nationalism." He campaigned for the return of the "Negro" to their ancestral land of Africa, and stressed the philosophy of "black pride." Making Africa more important and attractive to American Negroes, Garvey emphasized that the only hope for the Negro was to return to Africa. In this sense, he coined an instrumental slogan, "Africa for Africans," proclaiming himself the future provisional president of the Republic of Africa.[4]

With commitment to cultural nationalism, Garvey founded the Orthodox African Church and preached an African Christianity in which the very symbols of the Christian Church were domesticated to serve the African soul. For example, he preached that God and His angels are black and that Satan is white. As Benjamin Quarles explains: "In making the Negro feel that he was a somebody rather than a nobody, Garvey went to the extreme of becoming a black supremacist. In the African Orthodox Church he founded, angels were black and Satan and his imps were white, and the black worshippers could glorify 'the Black Man of Sorrows' and the 'Black Virgin Mother'."[5] In this sense, he became the spiritual ancestor of the present-day Black Muslim Movement. In fact, Elijah Mohammed (founder of the Black Muslim Movement) and Reverend Earl Little (Malcolm X's father), both were members of the uniformed corps of Garvey followers in the 1920s. [6] Garveyism--the philosophical and activist movement based on Garvey's teachings--became, in essence, the first black cultural nationalist movement in history to develop an international program to advance, socially and politically, the aspirations of black peoples.

Washington and Du Bois were the two other black leaders and intellectuals who exerted enormous influence on the Renaissance. Du Bois described succinctly that "Mr. Washington represents in Negro thought the old attitude of adjustment and submission...."[7] In the 1890s, Washington emerged as a black leader who championed the cause for "limited educational goals and separate social development" for his people. His Atlanta compromise speech of 1895,[8] embodied the thrust of his philosophy; in the South, "the radicals received it as complete surrender of the demand for civil and political equality; the conservatives, as generously conceived basis for mutual understanding."[9] The speech emphasized the need for blacks to acquire manual skills, to delve into the trades or, in short, to perfect their mastery of the use of the "hands." His philosophy was to eventually influence the notorious United States Supreme Court decision of 1896, known as *Plessy vs. Ferguson* which legalized public segregation on a "separate but equal" basis.[10]

Du Bois, however, rejected the accommodationist posture of Washington, providing an alternative in which he believed that blacks should aspire for the highest standards of intellectual excellence. Relegating blacks to only manual and technical training à la Washington's program, was to Du Bois, a plan of succumbing to the "slave mentality" which has often slowed black progress. He therefore opposed Washington's conciliatory attitude to white bait and mounted a robust defense of the cultivation of the black mind in the struggle to attain full civil rights for the "Negro." As he put it in that masterly *Souls of Black Folk* (1903):

> ...can there be any possible solution other than by study and thought and an appeal to the rich experience of the past? Is there not, with such a group and in such a crisis, infinitely more danger to be apprehended from half-trained minds and shallow thinking than from over-education and over-refinement?... We shall hardly induce black men to believe that if their stomachs be full, it matters little about their brains.[11]

Lest he be accused of intellectual high-mindedness, Du Bois was no naive daydreamer. He was a pragmatic visionary and an internationalist. To enhance the attainment of his objectives, he formed the National Association for the Advancement of Colored People; that is, the NAACP. (It should also be noted that immediately following the First World War; that is, in 1919, Du Bois and I. M. Blaise-Diagne, a black representative of Senegalese origin in the French government, called a Pan-African Congress in Paris which attracted fifty-seven delegates from Africa and from the black diaspora, drawing attention, then for the first time, to the common concerns affecting black peoples globally.) [12]

Between Washington and Du Bois, the latter's ideas contributed most to the birth of the Harlem Renaissance. Du Bois believed that the cream of the black crop, the most talented members of the race, what he called the "Talented Tenth," should obtain the best training in the high professions (such as law, medicine, and classics) and use their training to uplift their less fortunate kinsfolk.[13] In this sense, the black artistic talents which congregated in the mecca of Harlem, were a significant cultural force whose task was to use their art to promote black aspirations.

Perhaps Du Bois's most influential work around this time was *The Souls of Black Folk,* which was uncompromisingly direct and honest in its portrayal of the many disguises of slavery-bred American racism, its social and psychological impact on its beneficiaries and victims, and its particular harm on the "human condition" of the Negro, particularly in making the Negro strategically wear many faces as a coping tactic. The appearance of Du Bois's work was not well received by either whites or blacks who basked in contentment with the "uncle tomish" program of Washington and who therefore perceived Du Bois as a young troublemaker--a militant--who preached that the problem of the "twentieth century" was the problem of "the color line."[14] Du Bois employed his scholarly gift to explain the "double-consciousness" of the Negro which was manifest in his involuntary physical existence in America and his innate Africanness.[15] The Negro was a unity of historical tensions.

For the young talents of the Renaissance, Du Bois's scholarly, literary, and social contributions were just the right kind of inspiration which blacks needed. He inspired in them an informed pride rooted in a history which was as glorious and as flawed as that of the European's. The NAACP he created, published *The Crisis*, a journal which became a useful intellectual and pragmatic forum for creative and cultural expression by budding writers. Parallel to these efforts, Carter G. Woodson, another black Harvard Ph.D. like Du Bois--- as well as a graduate of the Sorbonne, also increasingly inspired the Renaissance artists by founding the *Association for the Study of Negro Life and History* in 1915, and the *Journal of Negro History* in 1916, which championed the study of Negro life, something which was, until then, largely the self-serving pursuit of whites--many with ulterior intentions, who pursued a self-congratulating coloring of history by rationalizing, as if "deserved," the Negro's inferior status.[16] The Negro, in short, was where he was because he deserved where he was!

Increasing access to educational opportunities contributed in no small measure to the critical mass of talents who were to congregate in Harlem. Preceding generations of black writers--harbingers like Phillis Wheatley (poet), Jupiter Hammon (poet), Charles Chesnutt (prose fiction), James Weldon Johnson (poet), and most eminently Paul Laurence Dunbar (poet), had already created a new literary tradition which the Renaissance writers only had to advance in a bold but massive direction.¹⁷ Impressively, the black talent that gathered in Harlem beckoned the call.

How would one define the birth of the New Negro Renaissance, and what was its special relation to Harlem from which it derived its name? "Renaissance," according to the French lexicographer Émile Littré, is a word "sometimes used to denote a lively movement in people's minds, after a period of oppression."¹⁸ Dr. Alain Leroy Locke, Harvard graduate and Oxford University Rhodes scholar, who also studied "philosophy, Greek and modern literature" at the University of Berlin and at the Collège de France and who was a professor of philosophy at Howard University---the most prominent intellectual—if not the doyen-- of the Renaissance, who, in fact, coined the term Negro Renaissance and campaigned for "the New Negro philosophy," used the term fittingly as the birth of a movement of cultural and artistic expression from an oppressed people who had much reason to dispel false myths, to combat old stereotypes, to abhor any return to bondage, to retrieve a smothered humanity, and to project a humane vision.¹⁹ Locke also edited a book of essays which is the seminal compilation of the ideas and spirit of the "Negro Renaissance."²⁰ The Harlem Renaissance was, in essence, a cultural revival, an attempt by African-Americans to show America that it, not them, needed to come of age; that the maturity of a nation was characterized by how well it lived up to the basic tenets of its social contract.

Harlem was very central to the "New Negro" movement, for in Harlem the "Negro" found solace with himself; it was as much a pilgrimage to a comforting place, the hub of New World black culture, the mecca of the black world, as it was a pilgrimage to the true African self.²¹ Harlem was an African journey in the mind, an asymptotic yearning to retrieve an African authenticity while still physically removed from Africa. Harlem was a black "melting pot," where blacks from the United States merged with their brethren from Africa, the West Indies, and Central and South America and acquired an awareness of racial unity and a cultural synergism which attracted national attention.²² Blacks from the rural South crossed the Mason-Dixon line and groped their way into Harlem where, according to Ralph Ellison, they had to change abruptly from being "a former cotton picker [to]... a surgeon."[23] In Harlem, as Marcus Hansen puts it, "what the son wishes to forget, the grandson wishes to remember." [24] In this sense, Harlem was not just a physical place; it was a metaphor for retrieving memory, for soul-searching into a relevant past.

The relevant past for the "Negro" was slavery with all of its brutal lessons and its impact on the psychology of both the self-proclaimed "master" and the prescribed "slave." The Renaissance was "a dialectical negation of slavery," where slavery is defined as "everything, whether *de facto* or *de jure*, which had aimed at robbing the Negro of his essential humanity."[25] The Renaissance "was to snatch off the mask" of the Negro imposed on him by slavery, to "show... his real face."[26] His real face was no longer that of the "sleeping Negro," the "Negro" wallowing in submissive passivity, but that of a full self-legitimizing human being who changed the hate and hurt of his experience into the refined sensibility of art. A culture-conscious art was the supreme achievement of the Renaissance and, indeed, its greatest contribution to American civilization. The Renaissance was both a negation and a construction. Alain Locke described it well that the Renaissance championed "the Negro's 'inner objectives' as an attempt to repair a damaged group psychology and reshaped a warped social perspective."[27] Its achievement was in creating a "new mentality for the American Negro." For in the drama, poetry, music, dance, and other arts of the Renaissance, there were profound expressions of the Negro's newly found self-consciousness and his self-assumed responsibility to be "somebody" in America. The "New Negro," in short and according to Ellison, stood firm to refute the old stereotypic and "hysterical forms of religion in alcohol and drugs."[28]

The New Negro's artistic movement thrived between 1922, up to the beginning of the Great Depression with the stock market crash of 1929.[29] Much of its trigger, as just discussed, was due to the crisis in the American South's rural economy (push factors such as the ravages of cotton boll weevil, floods, bad harvests, social terrorism as well as the pull factors of urban opportunities), resulting in the outmigration of blacks from the rural South to urban communities to work in industries to service World War I referred to as the Great Migration;[30] to their encounter with tough Jim Crow laws which influenced some of them to self-select into their own urban communities and, in New York, into the seemingly secure place of Harlem; to the inspiration from college-educated blacks largely in the North who found much enlightenment in their African and slavery past, and also to the patronage of liberal whites who flocked uptown to Harlem out of curiosity to sample the artistic delights largely performed before black audiences. White audiences and spectators patronized black jazz artists, musicians, and playwrights, whereas white publishers and patrons invested and profited from black talent and some, of course, did it just for the humanitarian thrill.[31]

Perhaps the most significant poets and writers of the Renaissance were Washington, D.C.-based Howard University professor, Dr. AlainLocke (1886-1954), Claude McKay (1890-1948), Jean Toomer (1894-1967), Langston Hughes (1902-67), and Countee Cullen (1903-46).[32] Mckay, Hughes, and Cullen were incontrovertibly the most significant poets. These artists made their significant contributions in poetry and in prose, albeit some of them were sometimes not hesitant to employ the common language of Negro music and/or the Negro dialect as legitimate media of artistic expression. Two magazines provided fora for enhancing the growth of the Renaissance writers: (1) *Opportunity* managed by Jessie Fauset and (2) *The Crisis* edited by Charles Johnson.[33] These periodicals, together with the persistent efforts of Locke, enriched the ground for the rich flowering of black talent. What were the poetic creations of the Renaissance which, *pari pasu*, contributed to American cultural maturity? The individual artistry of three of the major Renaissance poets suffices as exemplars.

As early as 1921, Cullen, a young "Negro" from Harlem's ghetto, published a poem in his high school magazine, *The Magpie*, of which he later became associate editor.[34] Six months later, Hughes, a high school graduate from Cleveland, Ohio, followed with the publication of his poem, "The Negro Speaks of Rivers," in *The Crisis*.[35] These young talents that attracted national attention for their works were bubbling with vitality and with deep historical consciousness. In 1922, McKay, a "Negro" immigrant from Jamaica, published a collection of poems titled, *Harlem Shadows*, which was equally impressive in its style and in its lyrical intensity, and in its purity of language and clearness of message.[36] *Harlem Shadows* consisted of the "quality of poems that Keats sought to cherish, when he said that 'Poetry should be great and unobtrusive, a thing which enters into the soul, and does not startle or amaze with itself but with its subject'."[37]

McKay's poetics, in particular, was stylistically impressive because of its strict adherence to conventional English metrical forms, especially the sonnet. Like James Weldon Johnson, McKay rejected the use of black vernacular and adhered to the discipline of standard English. He was already famous in England before his arrival in the United States in 1912.[38] He then had a stint at Tuskegee Institute and continued to Kansas State College studying agriculture, after which he proceeded to New York, where he performed a few menial jobs before proceeding full time into writing.[39] His poetry had "vigor and passion…; there is also tenderness of the most romantic sort."[40] One of McKay's most celebrated poems is, "If We Must Die," which is often singularly praised because it was quoted by Sir Winston Churchill in his speech to the U.S. Congress requesting American assistance in World War II.[41] The poem goes:

> If we must die, let it not be like hogs
> Hunted and penned in an inglorious spot,
> While round us bark the mad and hungry dogs,
> Making their mock at our accursed lot.
> If we must die, oh, let us nobly die,
> So that our precious blood may not be shed
> In vain; then even the monsters we defy
> Shall be constrained to honor us though dead!
> Oh, Kinsmen! We must meet the common foe!
> Though far outnumbered, let us show us brave,
> And for their thousand blows deal one death-blow!
> What though before us lies the open grave?

Like men we'll face the murderous, cowardly pack,
Pressed to the wall, dying, but fighting back![42]

This poem, apart from its fine artistry (with its deliberate choice of language and images, evocative marriage of rhyme with music, and restrained sentimentality) is a poem about heroism, designed to instill vigor into any cause where the proponents are materially weak but morally righteous. For blacks who were McKay's target-audience, the poem is essentially subversive artistry tailored to stir moral bravery and defiance against American racism and its attendant white monopoly of privilege. The sonnet was in fact written out of McKay's outrage over the flames of East St. Louis (where large number of black migrants from the South, faced with high rents and discrimination, caused race riots, and white mobs burnt homes and massacred in the black neighborhoods);[43] the lynchings of blacks in Houston, and the "Red Summer of 1919"— (so named by the black writer, James Weldon Johnson) (which, despite blacks after having fought valiantly for the United States in World War I, returned to find their country embroiled in one of the most intense periods of racial strife, with jobs few and competition for them intense. There were several black lynchings and some twenty-five race riots across the country in places such as Longview, Texas; Chicago, Illinois; Knoxville, Tennessee; Omaha, Nebraska, and Elaine, Arkansas, as lawless white supremacist vigilante groups like the Ku Klux Klan, sought to deprive blacks of the economic and social gains they have made).[44] Blacks, in return, mounted vigorous resistance. These events demonstrated to McKay that a socially relevant artist could not remain silent in the face of mindless brutality against his own people. Churchill's use of the poem as an appeal for help before the United States Congress was therefore peculiarly ironical-- perhaps a message of double talk—an ethically loaded "signifying" appeal.

A streak of bitterness and defensive anger generally characterized much of McKay's poetry, especially in poems like "Tiger," "The Negro's Tragedy," and "Enslaved." This is nowhere better illustrated than in these lines in "Enslaved":

> In the great life line of the Christian West;
> And in the Black Land disinherited,
> Robbed in the ancient country of its birth,
> My heart grows sick with hate, becomes as lead,
> For this my race that has no home on earth.[45]

The lines convey a sense of angry desperation, and should also be more forthrightly interpreted as the poet's rebellious musings against the intolerable conditions of his own people. Albert Camus describes this type of situation more aptly in *The Rebel* (1956):

> What is a rebel? A man who says no.... He is also a man who says yes, from the moment he makes his first gesture of rebellion. A slave who has taken orders all his life suddenly decides that he cannot obey some new command ...rebellion is founded... on the categorical rejection of...(the) intolerable and on the confused conviction of an absolute right.... Rebellion cannot exist without the feeling that, somewhere and somehow, one is right.[46]

In this sense, the existential unease which McKay felt for the intolerable condition of his people was something he had to rebel against through his most effective weapon; namely, his artistry.

There are, of course, some who would argue that political protest or belligerent poetry ruins a poet's art--the contention being that the poet who takes his art as a weapon for facile propaganda abandons the discipline and quest for beauty characteristic of the city of the muse—and embraces the city of the gun. But this type of argument is predictably suspect; for how can an artist whose every day life is distorted by the most absurd political atrocities, whose very imaginative existence is assaulted by stringent discriminatory laws and material squalor, whose own people confront daily the most absurd signals doubting the very essence for their existence, how can such an artist escape such realities and remain relevant? Rebellion therefore remains the very essence of valid art for it involves the artist engaging his circumstances, creating existential possibilities through the transcendental capabilities of the imagination. Alan Locke puts it well that, in McKay's poetry, we have "an intelligent realization of the great discrepancy between the American social creed and the American social practice forces upon the Negro the taking of the moral advantage that is his."[47]

One would do injustice to McKay, however, to characterize all of his poetry as defiant and rebellious. Some of his poetry was far from being belligerent. Some were indeed soul-searching and introspective, particularly his poems after his conversion from atheism to Catholicism. Consider his poem, "The Pagan Isms," which almost resembles a soul conversion:

> Around me roar and crash the pagan isms
> To which most of my life was consecrate,
> Betrayed by evil men and torn by schisms
> For they were built on nothing more than hate!
> I cannot live my life without the faith[48]

The poet became disillusioned with the soul-consuming cancer of secular pursuits; that is, the "pagan isms,"which he saw as being "built on nothing" but "hate." He reached a certain spiritual maturity where he was no longer fooled by the transience of material distinctions:

> And so to God I go to make my peace,
> Where black nor white can follow to betray.[49]

Here the biological distinctions of "black" and "white" become a non-category, a fortuitous happenstance, which conveys nothing to the poet but what the Hindus would call *maya* or "confusion." Race is a non-category precisely because it is pre-given and racism is a social construct, and race is not a reflection of achievement or of any innate capabilities on the part of the possessor. The historical conditioning which leads to the persecution of one race by another acquire a different meaning for the poet, a more elevated reexamination which leads him to see racial distinctions as suspect, and the only thing that really mattered for him then was to "make peace" with "God."

If McKay was the West Indian -born turned black American poet who started his poetry using the West Indian dialect and later became the master of the sonnet, then Langston Hughes was the black American poet who remained close to the deepest sensibilities of the American Negro, reflecting both the Negro's atavistic nostalgia for Africa, and the commonplace experiences and wisdom characteristic of the ways of black folk. Unlike Mckay and Weldon Johnson, Hughes, the more culturally relevant and prodigious talent, however, maintained his commitment to use the black metaphors of music (jazz and blues) and black folk wisdom to express his poetic soul.[50] Born in 1902 in Joplin, Missouri, Hughes spent his early years in Lawrence, Kansas; his father, who separated from his mother, was rich, whereas his mother was of moderate means. Hughes attended Columbia University, but his studies were aborted because of his father's refusal to finance it. He traveled to Africa and to Europe and, after publishing a few works, finished his education at Lincoln University with the support of a patron.[51] His poetry had a minimalist streak and was often informal.[52] Hughes published his first collection of poems, *The Weary Blues*, in 1926, after McKay published his *Harlem Shadows*. Hughes's first published poem, "The Negro Speaks of Rivers," when he was nineteen, depicted outright his resolution to the Negro problem of "double-consciousness." The poem is laced with muscular historicity weaved into brilliant incantatory rhythms:

> I've known rivers:
> I've known rivers ancient as the world and older than
> The flow of human blood in human veins.
>
> My soul has grown deep like the rivers.
> I bathed in the Euphrates when dawn were young.
> I built my hut near the Congo and it lulled me to sleep.
> I looked upon the Nile and raised the pyramids above it.
> I heard the singing of the Mississippi when Abe Lincoln
>   Went down to New Orleans, and I've seen it muddy
>   Bosom turn all golden in the sunset.
>
> I have known rivers:
> Ancient, dusky rivers.

My soul has grown deep like the rivers.[53]

The poem is characterized by the lyrical and imagistic longline reminiscent of the poetry of Walt Whitman. Raymond Smith notes that "unlike Whitman, however, who celebrated particular self ('Walt Whitman, the cosmos'), Hughes celebrated racial, rather than individual self. Hughes tended to suppress the personal element in his poetry, appropriating the first person singular as the fitting epitome of universal human tendencies embodied in race."[54]

Unlike Hughes, who was outgoing and socially engaged, Countee Cullen was another major Harlem Renaissance poet, who was reserved and inward-looking. He was described as "shy and withdrawn."[55] Cullen was born in 1903, in New York and schooled in Harlem and at DeWitt Clinton High School in the Bronx. He subsequently graduated from New York University and continued on to receive a master's degree in French from Harvard University, where he published his first book, *Color*.[56] He was extensively knowledgeable about traditional poetic forms "being at ease as a lyricist, an epigrammatist, and a narrative poet."[57] Margaret Perry notes that "the critics tended to play off Langston Hughes against Countee Cullen, praising the one and damning the other. ...The two young poets dominated the realm of black poetry during the decade of the the 1920s ...in essence, the traditional romantic aesthete (Cullen) and the genuine 'New Negro' (Hughes)...."[58] Cullen's interest and orientation toward the ninenteenth- century romantics, especially the work of John Keats,[59] became manifest in his own poetry which celebrated the "black man's grandeur."[60] In one of his classic poems, "Heritage," for example, he romanticized Africa with a dreamy poetic brush reminiscent of the Negritude poets:

> What is Africa to me:
> Copper sun or scarlet sea,
> Jungle star or jungle track,
> Strong bronzed men, or regal black
> Women from whose loins I sprang
> When the birds of Eden sang?
> *One three centuries removed*

From the scenes his fathers loved,
Spicy grove, cinnamon tree,
What is Afica to me?[61]

But the romancitization of Africa is "conflicted," as he struggles between the tensions of a Christian ubringing and the sensibilities and sensualities of a pagan past. As he later articulated in the same poem:

> Quaint, outlandish heathen gods
> Black men fashion out of rods,
> Clay, and brittle bits of stone,
> In a likeness like their own,
> My conversion came high-priced;
> I belong to Jesus Christ,
> Preacher of humility;
> Heathen gods are naught to me.[62]

The poet seems awed by the pagan mystery of Africa, the place of "spicy grove" and "cinnamon tree," and the place of "women whose loins he sprang," but that mystery is simultaneously dashed as "quaint" and as "outlandish" because it is a misleading worship of objects of human creation. Here, of course, Cullen succumbs to the ambivalence of the "brainwashing" effects of his Christian upbringing. Although his conversion to Christianity has come at a "high price" through the transplantation of his ancestors through slavery and through the struggle for racial equality, he seems "comfortable" with his eventual state for "heathen gods are naught [i.e., nothing] to him."

Switching back to Hughes, we encounter a poet whose work, apart from being emblematic of the movement, has had a more canonical influence on contemporary poetry than any other poet of the movement. Hughes's poetry combined three essential elements peculiar to the Renaissance's poetry: (a) a strong ancestry and ancestor consciousness in Africa (what critics called atavism); (b) a good consciousness and realism about the lives of ordinary black folk and the musicality of their language as exemplified in the blues, spirituals, and folk wisdom; and (c) a historical consciousness which conveyed a dignified sense of a rich cultural heritage and therefore of race pride. In *The Weary Blues* (1926), Hughes celebrates cabaret life and black history in Harlem.[63] This deep sense of history abounds in his works, as the following, "Poem," in *The Weary Blues* illustrates:

> We have tomorrow
> Bright before us
> Like a flame.
>
> Yesterday, a night-gone thing
> A sun-down name.
>
> And dawn today
> Broad arch above the road we came.
> We march![64]

This miniscule beauty is an imagistic reflection of the stages of history that the Negro went through. Hughes, as poet, is not ready to be bogged down with the past—the past is *past*; it has some important lessons, but it is a "night-gone thing"—"dawn-today" is an "arch" of opportunity in which the Negro must celebrate their triumph over racial oppression, but also be conscious of continuing to exercise agency in shaping an optimistic future. As the poet puts it in his poem, "We march!"

Notes

1. John Hope Franklin and Alfred A. Moss, Jr., *From Slavery to Freedom, Sixth Edition* (New York: McGraw-Hill Publishing, 1988): 238.
2. James Weldon Johnson, "Harlem: The Culture Capital," in *The New Negro: Voices of the Harlem Renaissance*, ed., Alain Locke (New York, Touchstone, 1997), 301.
3. Alain Locke, ed., *The New Negro, Voices of the Harlem Renaissance* (New York: Simon & Shuster, 1997): 6.
4. Alex Haley, *The Autobiography of Malcolm X as Told to Alex Haley* (New York: The Ballantine Publishing Group, 1999), 1-2.
5. Benjamin Quarles, *The Negro in the Making of America* (New York: Touchstone, 1987), 230.

6   Haley, *The Autobiography of Malcolm X*, 1.
7   W. E. B. Du Bois, *The Souls of Black Folk* (Nashville: The Fisk University Press, 1979), 50.
8   Ibid., 42-55.
9   Ibid, p. 43.
10 John Hope Franklin and Alfred A. Moss, Jr., *From Slavery to Freedom, Sixth Edition*, 238.
11 Du Bois, *The Souls of Black Folk*, 107.
12 George Padmore, ed., *History of the Pan-African Congress* (London: The Hammersmith Bookshop, 1963), 15.
13 Quarles, *The Negro in the Making of America*, 203.
14 W.E.B. Du Bois, *The Soul of Black Folk*, 40.
15 DuBois, *The Souls of Black Folk*, 3.
16 Ibid, 238.
17 William Stanley Braithwaite, "The Negro in American Literature," in *The New Negro: Voices of the Harlem Renaissance*, ed., Alain Locke (New York, Touchstone, 1997), 36-44.
18 Jean Wagner, *Black Poets of the United States: From Paul Laurence Dunbar to Langston Hughes* (Urbana: University of Illinois Press, 1973), 160.
19 Arnold Rampersad, "Introduction," in *The New Negro: Voices of the Harlem Renaissance*, ed. Alain Locke (New York: Touchstone, 1997), xi.
20 Ibid., xi.
21 Wagner, 154.
22 Alaine Locke, *The New Negro: Voices of the Harlem Renaissance*, 6-7; Wagner, *Black Poets of the United States: From Paul Laurence Dunbar to Langston Hughes*, 154-155.
23 Ralph Ellison, *Shadow and Act* (New York: Random House, Quality Paperback Book Club, 1994), 296.
24 Marcus Lee Hansen, *The Problem of the Third Generation Immigrant* (Illinois: Augustana Historical Society, 1938), 9.
25 Wagner, 167.
26 Ibid, 167.
27 Locke, 10.
28 Ellison, *Shadow and Act*, 298.
29 Rampersad, x-xix.
30 Wagner, 153.
31 Ibid, 174.
32 Ibid, 173.
33 Quarles, *The Negro in Making America*, 235-39.
34 Wagner, 287.
35 Wagner, 394.
36 Margaret Perry, *Silence to the Drums: A Survey of the Literature of the Harlem Renaissance* (West Port: Greenwood Press, 1976), 28-9.
37 Claude McKay, *Harlem Shadows: The Poems of Claude McKay* (New York: Harcourt, Brace and Company, 1922), xvii

38 Perry, 29.
39 Perry, 29.
40 Ibid.
41 Ibid.
42 Dudley Randall, ed., *The Black Poets: A New Anthology* (New York: Bantam Book, 1971), 63.
43 Wagner, 155.
44 John Hope Franklin and Alfred A. Moss, Jr., *From Slavery to Freedom* (New York: McGraw-Hill, 1988), 313-14.
45 Ibid., 62.
46 Albert Camus, *The Rebel* (New York: Alfred A. Knopf, 1956), 13.
47 Locke, 13.
48 Randall, *The Black Poets*, 64.
49 Ibid., 64.
50 Perry, 51.
51 Ibid., 46-47.
52 Quarles, *The Negro in Making America*, 235.
53 Ibid., 78.
54 Raymond Smith, "Hughes: Evolution of the Poetic Persona," in Harold Bloom, ed., *Langston Hughes: Bloom's Modern Critical Views* (New York: Chelsea Publishers, 1989), 49.
55 Quarles, *The Negro in Making America*, 235.
56 Perry, *Silence to the Drums*, 54-55.
57 Ibid., 235.
58 Margaret Perry, *Silence to the Drums*, 45.
59 Ibid, 54.
60 Perry, 54.
61 Randall, *The Black Poets*, 95.
62 Ibid., 97.
63 Perry, 50.
64 Alain Locke, "The New Negro," in Alain Locke, ed., *The New Negro: Voices of the Harlem Renaissance*, 5.

CHAPTER 9

THE EAGLE'S VISION: THE POETRY OF TANURE OJAIDE

Of the new generation of African poets and their poetry, there are only a few who one would read and return to. Nigeria's Tanure Ojaide belongs to those few. What makes Ojaide's poetry appealing is not only its technical qualities, but its cultural integrity. Ojaide is not the type of poet one remembers only by one good work; he is prolific, and his writings are consistently rich and deeply rooted in the Delta region of Nigeria. He has published more than five books of poetry, including *Children of Iroko and Other Poems* (1973), *Labyrinths of the Delta* (1988) *The Eagle's Vision* (1987), *The Endless Song*, and *The Fate of Vultures* (1990). If there is a persistent and unifying theme in most of his works, it is a single-minded detestation of tyrants combined with an obsessive commitment to social justice. This essay recognizes the impossibility of a deep exploration of this rising poetic star's work in a single foray (that, of course, would require treatment in a whole book) and therefore settles only for a brief, but ambitious survey of the artistry and social concerns of a poet who may very well be one of the finest, if not the finest, among Nigeria's harvest of poets of the post-Okigbo/post-Soyinka generation. The selection and treatment here of poems across many of the poet's several collections is adhoc and sporadic—the choice of poems largely motivated by a concern for representative demonstration. The treatment of Ojaide's work is undertaken within a meaningful triadic framework, rotating around three themes: his life, his artistry, and his social vision.

Born on April 24, 1948 in Okpara Island, Bendel State, Delta region of Nigeria, Ojaide thus grew up in this riverine forest area, largely brought up by his maternal grandmother, Amreghe, to whom he pays tribute in his poem, "For Granny." His formal education has generally been in Nigeria (at the University of Ibadan) and in the United States (at Syracuse University where he obtained his Ph.D.)—influences which cannot be taken lightly since the artistic mind is often a confluence of various intellectual and commonplace experiences. After graduate education at Syracuse, he taught for ten years at the University of Maiduguri, and subsequently taught as Visiting Johnston Professor of English at Whitman College in Walla Walla, Washington, and is now at the University of North Carolina in Charlotte.

Ojaide's writings have received several well-deserved praise from renowned poets and critics such as Hayden Carruth who states that he "may be one of the most important Nigerian poets of his generation."[1] He was a regional winner of the Commonwealth Poetry Prize in 1987, and has won other awards for his poetry including the Soyinka-endowed All-Africa Okigbo Prize for Poetry in 1988, and the BBC Arts and Africa Poetry Award, also in the same year.

But biodata and praise aside, what about Ojaide's artistry? Ojaide's poetry points *assegais* (a South African spear) at tyrants--the poem is simultaneously an "art form" and a "weapon" through which the "warrior-poet" confronts, criticizes, and condemns the political charlatanism and often deleterious role of African dictators. He is uncomfortable, as is evident in his poetics, with the retrogressive character of African leadership, who are often greedy, ruthless, and lacking in any coherent social vision and who, far from being benevolent, exploit the coercive authority of the state for often pernicious ends. His poems resemble what Soyinka, citing the poet Ted Joans, calls "shot-gun" poems—they are meant to be detonated immediately on the complacent bottoms of enemies. "Shot-gun" poems are aimed at a target—in Ojaide's case, "Africa's or Nigeria's malevolent dictators"—and they have a reason. This consuming theme of rebellion against tyranny and injustice, recurrent in much of his poetry, he has made inimitably his own. Take "The Fate of Vultures" where we get images stacked with insular density, representing the poet's powerful plea for accountability for public money from politicians who have gone hopelessly out of control, indeed beyond ministration:

> O Aridon, bring back my wealth
> From rogue-vaults;
> ....
> ...blaze an ash-trail to the hands
> that buried mountains in their bowels,
> lifted crates of cash into their closets.[2]

He equates the corrupt, self-gratifying breed of Nigerian politicians with "vultures," a biological symbol that is both ominous and sinister. But it is a contextually relevant symbol, implying both the disappearance of "life" and the appearance of political "carcass." In a sense, the withering away of classical public service, where the pursuit of the public good is perceived not only as individually wise but selfishly remunerative, has given birth to the stench of that sinister force—private greed. Ojaide is ready to call a "spade a spade," or more aptly, "a vulture a vulture," for he sees little virtue in obfuscating the ignoble scavenger-role of politicians in Nigeria's contemporary bodypolitic. For when those charged with duties for guarding our public patrimony abrogate their responsibilities, then society is forced to take notice. In this poem, Ojaide demonstrates, like Camus, that good poetic artistry must be inserted in the dramas of history, not as mere picture-postcard documentation, but as a mirror of those corrigible frailties of the human condition in the hope of alerting the "movers and shakers" of the Nigerian polity to do something about it.

There is, of course, the risk for poets to drop to the rhetorical commonplace when they wrestle with politics. But Lenard D. Moore of *The Small Press Review* is probably correct when he states: "Reflecting on the nature of society, Ojaide is careful not to confuse propaganda with art."[3] For in propaganda, the intent is to further one's cause by any means, even if it implies offending the public's sensibility with diffident clichés or, for that matter, compromising with bad artistry to promote a political point. In

Ojaide's works--political concerns abound, but they are handled with the reasoned devotion and care of a seasoned craftsman. The poet obviously demonstrates that he cannot afford the luxury of "art for art's sake," or pretty musings created to serve the genteel lifestyles of a moribund African parasitic class. He uses politics to invigorate his art, but is careful not to let his artistry suffer from political bad breath.

Ojaide is as much suspicious of politicians in those elevated seats of power as he is of people who feast on resources they did not work for. He believes that "freedom" for Africans carries with it a price which implies hard work, discipline, and commitment to moving society toward desirable social goals. So, he sings:

> You can tell
> when one believes freedom is a windfall
> and fans himself with flamboyance.
> The chief and his council, a flock of flukes
> gambolling in the veins of fortune.
> Range chickens, they consume and scatter....[4]

Empty flamboyance, to him, is a sign of lack of sincerity to self and to others. When powerful politicians steal public funds and waste, they violate the public's sacred trust. So, as a poet, he is ready to skillfully use poetic license to satirize the corruption under Nigerian presidents like Shehu Shagari. In a clever play of poetic pun, he contrasts ordinary Nigerians' deprivation of essential things like "food"-*gari*- and the billions of *nairas* which went into the building of Abuja with all of the attendant corruption in the allocation of contracts. As he puts it:

> Shamgari, Shankari, shun gari
> staple of the people
> and toast champagne;
> Alexius, architect of wind-razed mansions,
> a mountain of capital
> Abuja has had its dreams![5]

Why is it that former head of state Shagari and his cohorts shunned the basic needs of Nigerians-- Ojaide's *gari* (e.g., access to decent food, clean water, and shelter) and wasted the country's oil money on lavish imports (e.g., champagne, Mercedes Benzes, etc.) and on grand, unproductive public schemes nationwide (which Soyinka humorously ridiculed as the "Quadruple A": Ajaokuta steel mill, Abuja, Aluminium, and the Army). Wole Soyinka's instructive allusion to the propensity of Nigerians to find an easy scapegoat for their nation's economic woes in the long-serving finance minister, Alhaji Abubakar Alhaji (conveniently called "Triple A"), is revealing:

> Recently, in a quite incisive lecture delivered by a former Head of State, General Olusegun Obasanjo, the General related an encounter with a foreign Investor who had told him that the economic problem of Nigeria really did not have much to do with "Triple A" as with "Quadruple A." These quadruplets he then listed as Ajaokuta, Aluminium, Abuja and the Army. ...Ajaokuta...the...infamous steel rolling mill set up in partnership with the Soviet Union since 1973. Aluminium...another heavy-repercussion metallic pipe dream. Abuja...the soured, arid dream of a symbol of national unity, situated in the center of the country and the exit valve from the heart of the national treasury. The Army...of course—the Army. [6]

The poet, being an honest skeptic, thinks that political grandstanding has been pursued, in many cases, at the expense of the basic development of Nigerians. The pun with words such as "mountain of capital"—Abuja as a monumental "capital city" being by a mountain and a place where monumental public money was spent, shows the poet's shrewd ability to convey multiple meanings through the ambiguity of images. "Alexius" refers perhaps to Alex Ekwueme, then vice president, who, as an architect, was one of the major contractors who built Abuja.

But what is Abuja really? Could it be the elephant dreams of a nation with excess petrodollars (petro-*nairas*-- rather) gone sour? Or could it be a centrist concession—a megalopolis designed to assuage the bitter memories of a much villified (but perhaps redeeming) civil war? Abuja is perhaps both-- an elusive quest for the "true African soul" of Nigeria. We should concede that Nigeria is a domain of contrasts: black Africa's giant tormented by unresolved puzzles. Large and wealth-endowed, it has a dynamic and resourceful population. However, it suffers from some of the worst symptoms of the "big country syndrome." National cohesion is at best aspirational, and the country strives continuously to transcend the self-limiting, feet-shooting defeatism of ethnicity. An ethos of "cheat or risk being out-cheated" has crystallized since independence, which has made public trust and public good words only in the lexicon of idealists. Lagos-- that quintessential mirror of what is wrong with Nigeria—squalor and the individual disparities in wealth and in social status, ethnic disharmony disguised into religious and sectarian tensions, degenerate opportunism reinforced by a self-seeking social ethics, and a rowdy but humorous and open attitude to self-criticism-- all of these made it necessary, if nothing else, for Nigeria was to opt for a fresh lease on progressive nationhood. A new capital perhaps serves as a first step. Surely, Abuja--despite all of the waste which went into her construction--could serve the real need for unity of a potentially great nation.

In what appears to be my favorite of Ojaide's poems; that is, "Where Everybody Is King," we are confronted with a theme which has a larger significance for contemporary Africa. The setting of the poem is Agbarha, and the poet employs the lyrical qualities of traditional Urhobo poetry (the ethnic group from which he hails) to shed light on some self-defeating attitudes characteristic of some contemporary Africans:

> Come to Agbarha
> where everybody is king
> and nobody bows to the other.
> Who cares to acknowledge age, since
> power doesn't come from wisdom?
> And who brags about youth
> when there's no concession to vitality?
> You just carry your head high.

> And do you ask why
> where nobody accepts insults
> doesn't grow beyond its petty walls?[7]

The humor of the poem is in its sarcasm. The Urhobo town of "Agbarha" could be any place in Africa--it is a symbolic place of "larger Africa" writ small. The poet, in some sense, laments contemporary African attitudes which show no respect for traditional African authorities and institutions. Foolish pride becomes very self-destructive if it does not make concession to the wisdom of elderly experience and to the vitality of youths.

The poet is even more pointed in his public indictment of the indolence of his people when he states:

> When you come to Agbarha
> mind you, the town of only kings,
> there are no blacksmiths, no hunters;
> you will not find anybody
> doing menial jobs that will
> soil the great name of a king--
> nobody ever climbs the oil-palm
> nor taps the rubber tree.
> Everybody is as bloated
> as a wind-filled bag.[8]

In short, foolish pride--Ojaide's "wind-filled bag"—is no substitute for humility to one's manual trade and hardwork. This could, of course, be said for many places in Africa where the culture of consumption has outstripped that of production, resulting in a grave economic and social crisis in the continent. Ojaide sees that some parts of contemporary Africa are "basket cases" precisely because the precolonial attitudes of hardwork, fending for oneself, and engaging in food production and artisan activities have increasingly been unfortunately displaced by a dangerous craving for consumerism and flamboyance. The role of the state and some external "do-gooders" have not, many times, helped either, by their adverse policies and actions, which have served to tax heavily rural producers to appease politically more vocal urban consumers.

The imagery, the terseness of the message, and the humor--all point to Ojaide's view that even dignity has to be earned. In short, there is a contradiction between many an African's quest for self-respect and for their outer penury. Africans would have to work hard to build viable and relevant educational institutions; they should not settle for an easily assumed self-dignity, for the rest of the world will not grant respect easily. In Ojaide's own lines:

> In Agbarha
> nobody wakes to work;
> everybody washes his mouth with gin
> and sits at home
> on a floor-mat of a throne.
> Are you surprised
> at kwashiorkor princes and princesses,
> prostitute queens and beggar kings?
> Come to Arbarha
> where everybody prides himself greater
> than the rest of the world
> and see the hole
> where kings live their unfortunate lives.[9]

The images are stacked with cultural accuracy, contradictory in their suggestion, ebullient in their richness. The world of "prostitute queens" or "beggar kings" is a world in which reality is revolting and dignity is more aspirational than real.

What these poems demonstrate, as indeed most of Ojaide's poetry, is that his artistry is largely informed by a deep and unabashed interest in the events and direction of his society. In this sense, the poet is not ashamed to evoke images from within his own local universe. Corrupt politicians and their religious coconspirators take carnivorous traits—"hyenas" or "vultures," or the poet retrieves murderous tyrants such as "Ogiso" from his Urhobo past and transposes their roles to fit modern tyrants. Godwin Ede, in an issue of *The Guardian* (1991), had this to say:

> Though a sleepy god, the poet sometimes heeds that call to home and hearth and makes ready fire-wood to warm the people

out of their anxieties. Tanure Ojaide has succeeded in such a populist application of himself. He is relevant and down-to-earth. In his BBC prize-winning poem, "The fate of vultures", he remonstrates with the fugitive politician: "O Aridon, bring back my wealth from rogue vaults...." His "song" is the "...music of communal pain...."[10]

Ede is correct about the contextual relevance of Ojaide's artistry in much the same way many critics have spoken of the down-to-earth relevance of Chinua Achebe's artistry to Iboland, Nigeria, and to larger Africa. In some sense, "relevance" is often a backhanded way of saying that a writer constructs from his roots and indeed produces something of great social significance.

In Ojaide's poetry, one is often struck by the broad latitude of the themes he treats, from the problems of environmental degradation in the Sahel, to the issues of the persecution of Jews by Nazis, to black suffering under American white racism. In a poem titled, "In the Sahel," he describes with poignant accuracy, the fate of the peoples living near the Sahara Desert: "I am witness to the sun-drunk fate/....Dust has dressed me in its fashion, powdered...there's no independence, since I am the colony of charities."[11] The effects of population pressure on limited cultivable land is increasingly translating into the loss of grass and tree cover, as poor families scrape for firewood and charcoal and places to grow food. This, of course, has been made worse by declining and erratic rainfall in much of particularly Sahel-Africa, leading to an "ecological wasteland"—poet Ojaide's well-put "sun-drunk fate." The people of the Sahel, indeed, have more sun than their survival can bear, inheriting a Bangladesh of the sun! But Ojaide is skeptical about international responses to the Sahelian drought which he sees as nothing but a new form of colonialism. For him, the seemingly benign act of international charity carries with it malignant consequences in the form of dependency, undermining of local initiative, and loss of a dignified human face.

In an interesting twist to the claim of Jewish crucifixion of Christ, Ojaide takes a different perspective in his poem:

To this day

> the Romans insult our intelligence--
> their Governor washed off his hands
> and the Jews killed Jesus.[12]

This poem has greater implications and shows Ojaide's general distrust of centers of power, who may indeed trick populations into believing what has no corroborative support. As he puts it:

> We know
> how they plant evidence
> to incriminate innocent ones,
> who suffer untold misery
> for what they never did....[13]

For Ojaide, the suffering of African peoples is linked to the suffering of other human beings; hence the "hyenas" and "vultures" of history who perpetrate such anguish must be exposed and, if need be, challenged and booted out. There is a recognition throughout his poetry that concentrations of power combined with ignorance can, if unchecked by enlightened opposition, have lethal consequences.

In a poem titled "New Orleans" about that city demonstrating his general sympathy with the conditions of blacks in America, he sings:

> Eddie's Restaurant always full.
> The architecture so Catholic, Spanish and Black.
> The eternal French Quarter--Bourbon Street
> bubbling with sex and trombones at night.
> And the Mississippi, that huge snake of water!
> As I sailed with memories of distant days
> I passed abandoned quays and relics of pain.[14]

There is a strong awareness of the way in which place conveys a deep sense of history; the architecture, Bourbon Street, the Mississippi--all bring back to the poet memories of distant days. Place in this sense coincides with time, and place marks a certain emotional temperament, captures a certain state of the world, which the poet, in empathy with the precise condition of his race in America, characterizes as "relics of pain." What makes this poem artistically rich, reminiscent in many ways of Langston Hughes, is the way in which images of place are synchronized with events in time to convey a lively scene, bubbling with the vernacular-smell and gusto of New Orleans cabaret life.

Sometimes the poet's concern is very particular and pedestrian as in the poem, "Ughelli," where the "...image of the people exploited and discarded is central... where Ughelli, a town in the oil belt of Nigeria represents the owner neglected and dying of need when her possession helps make others comfortable":[15]

> To see her dry-skinned when her oil rejuvenates hags
> to leave her in darkness when her fuel lights the universe
> to starve her despite all her produce
> to let her dehydrate before the wells bored into her heart
> to have her naked despite her innate industry
> to keep her without roads when her sweat tars the outside world...
> and for her to be sucked anaemic by an army of leeches,
> it is a big shame.[16]

The poetic device Ojaide uses here is one of repetitive listing of an idea through a menu of images, the lines are Walt Whitmanesque in style and convey a litany of complaints, and the meters leap like a snake with a dismembered spine. The poet's eventual position of utter disgust is summed up in his last line which is a cliché of common speech: "It is a big shame."

In the balkanized national politics of independent Nigeria, the poet sees that ethnicity and regionalism exact their self-serving prices: the Yoruba and the Ibo and, above all, the Hausa monopolize the seats of economic and political power and have increasingly used it to drain areas like the Delta region into "fourthworld areas" whereas their own regions have been built to support the leisure lifestyles of an aspirational "second world." The Ibo, who exhibit tremendous entrepreneurial skills, have in many ways sometimes suffered persecution for their enterprise. The literary genius Chinua Achebe captures this reality in *The Trouble with Nigeria* in more exacting terms:

> Nothing in Nigeria's political history captures her problem of national integration more graphically than the chequered fortune of the word *tribe* in her vocabulary. *Tribe* has been accepted at one time as a friend, rejected as an enemy at another, and finally smuggled in through the back-door as an accomplice. ...In Nigeria, in spite of our protestations, there *is* plenty of work for *tribe*.[17]

And for ethnic groups like the Urhobo in the Delta region, powerlessness becomes a self-negating feature as alliances are forged with more dominant ethnic groups in the Nigerian polity who may very well be really hostile and yet put on the altruistic ethnic guise of big brother patronage. Achebe's advice for a more neutral and progressive role for the Nigerian state is prophetic: "although we may not be able to legislate prejudice and bigotry out of the hearts and minds of individual citizens, the state itself and all its institutions must not practice, endorse or condone such habits."[18]

If much of Ojaide's poetry revolves around political themes, there are some poems which are refreshingly personal and show that the poet is as much capable of the "broad political brush" as of the little concerns of "humane touch." Consider "A Verdict of Stone," which is a poetic tribute to the poet's maternal grandmother Amreghe, who brought him up:

> As I walk down the ruin of old blocks
> into homes built on dead bones,
> I know you were
> *Ayayughe* of the tales,
> gathering firewood after every storm;
> pounding yam for the little ones.[19]

The poet sees the grandmother as a constructive force, the powerful feminine ground on which his own life was built. The grandmother was a nurturer, a gem of enormous strength, who, according to the poet, weaned many mouths:

> No doors open where you weaned
> a dozen mouths who swung you here and there;[20]

Ojaide is even more sentimental in the last stanza of the poem where he sees his grandmother's life work as a monumental contribution to earth's song:

> In your flitting twilight, you called
> my name with your last breath,
> and I held you; but you were already
> irrevocably possessed for the endless journey.
> Today I call your name, *Amreghe*,
> with an elephant tusk;
> the island vibrates with your music.[21]

The poet is both sad and celebrative: the death of his grandmother does not translate into a meaningless end--she continues to live in the hearts and minds of those she raised, in the good works she left behind.

Overall, Ojaide's artistry can be surmised as pivoting around the themes of protestation against political and economic tyranny, and he does so with a deep sense of rootedness in his Delta region and in Urhobo culture in particular, evoking sometimes both mythical and commonplace characters and images, and never letting his sense of place degenerate into a universal despair. His poetry is often lyrical, informed by the musical traditions of the Urhobo. He does not indulge in the poetic pretensions of the earlier generation of African poets, in their use of archaisms, suppression of verbal linkages, rhyme, exotic words and images, neurotic self-consciousness, and other poetic idiosyncrasies characteristic of the European models of their colonial education. He instead uses the language of prose, employing "traditional African folk `literary' techniques."

Quoting from his own essay, Ojaide, like most of the new generation of African poets, is "public in his treatment of themes, conscious of an audience, is unpretentious, clear and simple in expression. In fact, he is `unpoetic' in the old way because he employs the syntax of prose. Because it is a speaking voice, the poetry flows, unlike the occasionally stilted poetry of Clark and Soyinka."[22] He evokes the ghosts of such mythical heroes as Ogiso (the Delta tyrant) and Shaka (the Zulu tyrant) but refurbishes their image to project a more humane future.

And this brings me to a brief discussion of Ojaide's social vision. Does he indeed have one? A critic had this to say:

> Ojaide is like many Nigerian poets who have written before him with respect to his view on the relationship between literature and history. Like Okigbo, Soyinka, Okara, his poetry takes off from the present in desperate search for values to redeem its malaise. The search takes him to the immediate past in the history of colonialism, and beyond that into the pre-colonial ancestral history and culture. He differs from Soyinka in his view of history... as recurring cycles of bestiality...Ojaide believes it is possible to move history forward through progressive regeneration.[23]

Without endorsing whether the critic provides an accurate portrayal of Soyinka's position and taking that purely as red herring and therefore incidental to this essay, his view of Ojaide's social vision is nonetheless correct. Ojaide consistently believes there is some useful energy in the past which could revitalize the present and move us into a future. As one of his poems illustrates:

> Now fight your way back
> to help us in these desperate days.
> Shame on gods who look on, bemused
> as lightning strikes their devotees
> in their own groves.[24]

The poem is titled "Future Gods" and it resonates with an important lesson which is that history must not be read from the sidelines. History requires and commands involvement, in learning from its savage lessons and receiving inspiration from its high moments. Perhaps it is this sober view of an active humanity able to learn and change positively the course of history which makes Ojaide an optimistic poet whose view of life is enormously refreshing.

Notes

1. Tanure Ojaide, *Labyrinths of the Delta* (New York: The Greenfield Review Press, 1990), blurb.
2. Ojaide, *The Fate of Vultures and Other Poems* (Lagos, Nigeria: Malthouse Press, 1990), 11.
3. Ibid., blurb.
4. Ibid., 11.
5. Ibid., 11-12.
6. Wole Soyinka, "Culture, Memory, and Development," Keynote address in *Culture and Development in Africa*. Eds. Ismail Serageldin and June Tabroff (Washington, DC: The World Bank, 1992), 215.
7. Ojaide, *The Fate of Vultures and Other Poems*, 58.
8. Ibid., 58.
9. Ibid., 59.
10. Godwin Ede, "Is Poetry a Dying Genre?" *The Guardian*, 8, no. 5 (October 5, 1991),17.
11. Ojaide, *Eagle's Vision* (Michigan: Lotus Press, 1987), 19.
12. Ibid., 21.
13. Ibid.
14. Ibid., 23.
15. Aderemi Bamikunle, "Literature as a Historical Process: A Study of Ojaide's *Labyrinths of the Delta*," in *African Literature and African Historical Experience*, eds. Chidi Ikonne, Emelia Oko, and Peter Onwudinjo (Ibadan: Heinemann Nigeria, 1992), 77.
16. Ojaide, *Labyrinths of the Delta*, 74.
17. Chinua Achebe, *The Trouble with Nigeria* (Enugu, Nigeria: Fourth Dimension Publishing,1983), 5.
18. Ibid., 7.
19. Ojaide, *Labyrinths of the Delta*, 58.
20. Ibid.
21. Ibid.
22. Ojaide, "The Changing Voice of History: Contemporary African Poetry," *Geneve-Afrique*, 27, no.1 (1989), 115.
23. Bamikunle, "Literature as a Historical Process," 81.
24. Ojaide, *The Endless Song* (Lagos, Nigeria: Malthouse Press, 1989), 52.

CHAPTER 10

AN ENTIRE STAR HAS LEFT US: CHINUA ACHEBE, IN MEMORIAM

I will miss Chinua Achebe. His passing away is as if an entire constellation-star has collapsed. It is monumental, weighty, concerning, depriving, and sad.

It is monumental because it is difficult to imagine African literature without Achebe. He was one of African literature's most ardent champions and undoubtedly one of its great contemporary voices. Achebe is by no means the first African novelist; there have been antecedent novelists like the South African Thomas Mafolo, who wrote *Pitseng* (1910) and *Chaka* (1925). He is not the first Nigerian novelist; there has been Amos Tutuola, who wrote the *The Palm Wine Drinkard* (1953), which the Irish poet Dylan Thomas, described as a "grisly and bewitching story, written in young English by a West African...."[1] Thomas was alluding, in typical imperial condescension, that Tutuola's story was "primitive" and that his English was "young"—it still had some way to grow. If one goes narrower, Achebe is not even the first Igbo novelist; there has been Pita Nwana, who published *Omenuko* (1933) in Igbo, which won the Africa-wide competition in indigenous African languages.[2] Achebe is not even the first Igbo novelist who wrote in English; there has been Cyprian Ekwensi, who published *People of the City* (1954). The significance of Achebe, I would argue, is that he was a cultural revolutionary figure in the same way that Albert Einstein was revolutionary for science. He led a paradigm change in African literature, which was that Africans did not have to imitate Europeans to tell their own stories. They could use European languages to expand their audience, but they must tell their stories as Africans in the same way that Europeans tell their stories as Europeans. Chinweizu and his Bolekaja group of critics put it succinctly: "And Achebe's Things Fall Apart was, as he himself have often said, a deliberate (and successful effort) to recreate a pre-Westernized African reality, using authentic Igbo characters, situations, values, and religious concepts, and bending the English Language to express Igbo proverbs and idioms."[3] Achebe set the foundations for an African storytelling that was to be done as simply and unapologetically truthful as possible, drawing on the rich repertoire of Africa's traditions and environment, and using and bending European languages only as tools to facilitate the conveying of their stories, but not getting trapped or seduced by their self-alienating aspects.

And there rests the monumental greatness of Achebe. That a young man in his late twenties in 1958, would, through the singular effort of his first novel, *Things Fall Apart*, eclipse artistically all of his predecessors and switch the curiosity of a world that has been long accustomed to Europeans or Arabs defining Africans, to Africans now defining themselves with a language that was laced with existential profundity, marrying comedy and tragedy, and conveying deep oral traditional richness. Achebe has often said that one of the things he has tried to do in his work was to switch Europe's long domineering monologue into a dialogue. Europe has been talking, talking for a long time. Europe has been talking to non-Europeans everywhere, and often talking down to them. Europe has been interpreting the histories of non-Europeans and defining others through its self-aggrandizing own frame of reference. Achebe saw this as problematic. The rest of the world did not only have ears to take orders, they also had mouths to express themselves. It was important to force Europe to pause from its long, uninterrupted speech and listen. Achebe's *Things Fall Apart* was a brave and successful effort in that direction. It was the empire writing back. It was the empire speaking back not as a defensive response as Negritude uncritically became, but as a parallel conversation. You have your stories; we have ours. We can learn from each other's stories.

Many Africans identify with Obi Okonkwo, Achebe's tragic protagonist, in *Things Fall Apart*, because Okonkwo spoke something deep about African's inner yearnings and sensibilities. He stood up for the right to defend the indigenous autochtonous. He remained firm, despite the fact that his village accommodated and made compromises with the colonial invader and eventually abandoned him in the lurch. Although Achebe sees Okonkwo's inflexibilities to adapt to the intrusion of empire as what eventually led to his downfall, he makes us love and admire this indigenous hero. He eulogizes Okonkwo through Obierika, "That man was one of the greatest men of Umuofia. You drove him to kill himself, and now he will be buried like a dog...."[4] Colonialism reversed the social order of indigenous African communities; the great got socially demoted and the not-so-great got elevated. Colonialism also injured the African mind and spirit, but Africa was far too resilient to go down. Africans have cultural roots deep as baobabs. They mustered the ability to heal and to rebuild. Speech was part of the rebuilding. Achebe's storytelling was, in short, that of a freedom fighter. Like the Jamaican Reggae world star Bob Marley, who surreptitiously graced us in his songs, "Get Up, Stand Up. Stand Up for Your Rights," Achebe graced us in his stories to speak out what is valuable in our midst.

Achebe is monumental because he believed in speech—especially by and for Africans, and saw how peoples who are speech-deprived or who have others speaking for them, can find themselves mentally slaving in the alphabet soup of the dispossessor. All free peoples have to reclaim their stories and to speak for themselves. Achebe was clear about this in his 2002 speech as winner of the German Peace Prize, awarded by the German Book Trade. He concluded: "The Africa I write about is not inhabited by people without speech. I grew up hearing sometimes magnificent, and always efficient, language in my community. I did not hear the grunts and the screeches that savages were supposed to use instead of speech. So, I wrote what

I did hear, in a translation that accorded equal respect to the two languages I have."[5] And Achebe is right. My people, the Wolof, have a saying, *Wakh moi nit* or literarily, *"Speech is the person."*

It is irrefutable that the whole project of empire was partly based on the propagation of myths of superiority through stories, and partly on deeds to promote the interests of empire, some of it based on violence or on the threat of violence in the event of native resistance. Natives were classified into a hierarchy of beings. Those with written narratives were superior to those strictly oral. The latter were considered primitive and without history. Hugh Trevor-Roper, then Regius Professor of History at Oxford, one of the more learned men of Europe at the time, was not learned enough to give Africa its due appraisal. The manuscripts *Tarikh al-Sudan* and the *Tarikh al-Fattash* and the over half a million other manuscripts of the civilizations of ancient Mali/Timbuktu, the *Kibre Negest*, and other *geis* manuscripts of Ethiopia were all not within his zone of awareness, or were deliberately ignored, to result in his ignorant assertion in his 1964 book, *The Rise of Christian Europe*: "Undergraduates, seduced, as always, by the changing breath of journalistic fashion, demand that they should be taught the history of black Africa. Perhaps, in the future, there will be some African history to teach. But at present there is none, or very little: there is only the history of Europeans in Africa. The rest is largely darkness… And darkness is not a subject for history."[6]

Trevor-Roper did not moderate his "sins" with informed scholarship; he rode on his imperial highhorse with the scholarship of a maxim gun: "If all history is equal…we may neglect our own history and amuse ourselves with the unrewarding gyrations of barbarous tribes in picturesque but irrelevant corners of the globe…."[7] But, in retrospect, should we not amuse ourselves with the scholarship of Trevor-Roper? For, if scholarship is about truth-finding and about truthtelling, should it not have occurred to a seemingly bright mind as Trevor-Roper to search deeper for evidence to back his arguments? Is scholarship about making untutored speculative claims? The magnificence of Achebe is that he challenged such

European storytellers and mythmakers as Hugh Trevor-Roper, Joseph Conrad, Count Joseph Arthur de Gobineau, and Georg Wilhelm Friedrich Hegel. They were bright men but limited by the prejudices of their education and by their environment. They were raised during the period of the great European imperialisms and bought into the imperial project; hence, they became facilitators or propagators of narratives of denigration of the "other." They spread not truth and understanding, but self-serving narratives and myths of cultural superiority.

I will miss Achebe because his passing away is weighty. Achebe was not, by any means, a prolific writer; five novels and one collection of short stories is a lean harvest for a major writer. However, Achebe's achievement is not in the quantity of his oeuvres, but in their quality. I have noted in our biography on him, *Chinua Achebe: Teacher of Light*, that his works are "deceptively simple and accessible and so richly interlaced with Igbo proverbs that they have the rare classical elegance of Biblical parables."[8] Achebe saw himself first and foremost as a teacher, but not as your "beat me down" teacher of today's crash schools, but a great teacher, like a Gandhi or Confucius, of African and Third World literatures. This is because of the sheer moral weight of Achebe's literary productions. His writings have an enduring, pedagogic quality. My good friend, the late professor Emmanuel Obiechina (Achebe's friend also) and one of the most humble and decent Nigerians I have ever encountered, once remarked to me about the weight of Achebe's moral authority in the popular discourse of Nigerians, "Many a time in popular palaver that only Nigerians know how--- Chinua Achebe is quoted to support or illustrate a point. His words are like the palm oil with which the words are eaten."

Achebe's contribution to the early development of modern African literature is not only qualitatively enormous, but hinges on the legendary. When his first novel, *Things Fall Apart*, made a breakthrough with Heinemann Publishers in 1958, Heinemann made him the founding editor of the Heinemann African Writers Series, in which he oversaw the development of the entire African continent's literature. He edited the first hundred titles.

His enormous self-sacrifice in reviewing and in commenting on even the worst manuscripts took much valuable time from his own creative work, but undoubtedly helped in the shaping of the continent's literature. Even after editing his last title for Heinemann, Achebe continued to mentor and to encourage young writers through his University of Nigeria-Nsukka literary publication, *Okike,* and through other avenues. As Achebe became an elder and began to cope with a debilitating physical condition, he began to understandably cut down on his social engagements. In 2003, I made a phone request to Achebe about writing a blurb for a promising first novel by a young Nigerian novelist. In his characteristic polite and forthright manner, Achebe replied, "Thank you. But I have already done my national service." We laughed over the matter—especially the use of the term "national service" –reflecting mandatory youth service by the Nigerian government. I reflected on the response, and said, yes, he was right. He had sacrificed enough for the cause of Africa's literary development and it was his time to rest. Others now needed to step in and to fill the void.

Achebe's legendary status accompanied the popularity of his novels. I recalled a two-hour evening encounter with the Egyptian Arab 1988 Nobel Laureate, Naguib Mahfouz in 1998, at Farah Boat in Cairo, Egypt. The meeting was organized by Amr Shaarawi, a professor of electrical engineering at Cairo University, who had been a graduate school friend of mine. Amr Shaarawi, I later learned, was the grandson of Huda Shaarawi, the first Egyptian feminist woman to remove the veil. Huda Shaarawi has a street named after her near the currently fabled prodemocratic protests venue, Tahrir Square. In any case, when we met Mahfouz, he wore dark glasses and seemed to continuously smile and to stare up, in the manner of the African-American singer Ray Charles, as if he was blind. I asked Mahfouz whether he was familiar with African literature south of the Sahara. He gave a bemused response, noting that he remembered in the sixties, when Gamal Abdel Nasser championed Pan-Africanism (with his friend Osagyefo Kwame Nkrumah) that he read a fascinating book written by a Nigerian which the translator noted as, *When Things Go Down*. He was referring to *Things Fall Apart*. Achebe's novel was famous, even in Egypt. I informed Achebe about this encounter, and he seemed amused by the twist in the title of his novel. We laughed about it over the phone.

Achebe's passing away is weighty in another respect. He was not only a great writer; he was a builder of African cultural institutions. In 1989, I received a letter from him, asking me to serve on the Editorial Board of *African Commentary: A Journal of People of African Descent*, a new Pan-African magazine that he founded while he was a visiting professor at the University of Massachusetts in Amherst. I accepted the invitation. The core drivers of the magazine were the distinguished Nigerian engineer, Bartholomew Nnaji, who was then director of the Automation and Robotics Lab at the University of Massachussetts--- and who later became the minister of science and technology in the short-lived Nigeria government of Ernest Shonekan and then subsequently served as minister of energy in the federal government of President Goodwill Jonathan. Nnaji had been a graduate school colleague and friend. The editiorial board also included other prominent individuals, such as Okey Ndibe, Chudi Uwazurike, Obi Nnaemeka, John Maxwell, Michael Mbabuike, and C. Don Adinuba and such intellectual/public heavyweights as Ali A. Mazrui, Dennis Brutus, A. M. Babu, Leonard Jeffries, Nadine Gordimer, Olusegun Obasanjo, Michael Thelwell, Chinweizu, Ibrahim Gambari and Fela Anikulapo-Kuti. What was Achebe's vision with this magazine, which had debut editions pitched at such a high level of journalism? So impressive, the magazine got even compared to *The New Yorker*. Achebe's vision for the magazine was part Africa gloriana, part restoration, but more importantly, it was a forum for Africans and for people of African descent to reflect and to devise joint solutions to the current ills confronting the continent. Achebe's editorial in the debut edition summed it all:

> Africa is more than a geographic reality; it is a spiritual phenomenon, born truly enough, of a painful history--- the

history of slavery—but it is a history which binds every Black person to Africa. It is for this reason that *African Comentary* is a "a journal of for people of African descent"—whether they are African Americans, or Africans in Europe, the Caribbean, or in the homeland.

It is not too long to the 21st century: we are indeed running out of time. The goal of *African Commentary* is, in part, to ensure that Africa and the rest of the Black world step into the next century, with dignity and a restored sense of initiative. In the decades since many African nations became independent, the question of forging African unity has often been raised and sabotaged by African leaders themselves. With just about ten years to the 21st century, it is clear for us that Africa cannot make it on the individual steam of the diverse countries.

African Commentary is committed to reclaiming the rich heritage of Africa, and re-drawing the contours of African history. Beyond reclaiming the African past, the pages of African Commentary will be open to some of the best minds in Africa and the Black world to ponder the question of Africa's and its descendants place in the world today.[9]

With this preamble, Achebe was on an ambitious intellectual project. The high quality of the essays in the magazine were difficult to sustain without resources. Unfortunately, *African Commentary* lasted between 1989 and 1992, and then morphed into *African World* in 1993, and then went defunct due to inadequate funding. The thin subscription base, the weak advertisement mobilization, and the inability to develop an endowment aborted its growth.

The "bug" to build cultural institutions, however, has continued in Achebe's eldest son, Ikechukwu (fondly called Ike), a Cambridge University doctorate, who quietly has continued to do many important cultural projects for the development of Africa. Ike, for example, was a major force in having Rosen Publishing House of New York start the Library of African Peoples, a series of monographs on Africa's major ethnic groups targeted to young adults. In fact, through Ike's foresight, I was asked and I wrote an ethnography on the Wolof peoples of

Senegal and The Gambia, which appeared in the Rosen series. Moreover, Ike has been busy developing the Chinua Achebe Foundation as well as leading a project for the preparation of an Igbo archival dictionary. Although funding for this has been tough to come by, Ike has been persistent and is slowly making headway.

I have always been puzzled about why so few Africans with money support the development of African cultural institutions. Whereas America, in its early development, has seen the Vanderbilts, the Dukes, the Carnegies, the Mellons, the Fords, and the Rockefellers use their largesse to support higher educational, scientific, and artistic institutions; in Africa, the capitalist class has continued to be largely and shortsightedly parasitic and only a few visionary and philanthropic. One could point to a few like the late Nigerian chief Bashorun Abiola, who financed African magazines, such as the *African Concord*, and supported chairs in universities and lectureships in academic associations, such as the African Studies Association; and perhaps, the Sudanese Mo Ibrahim, who sponsors the Mo Ibrahim Index and governance indicators, and the Mo Ibrahim Prize for African leaders who practice good governance and exit power voluntarily. But even these well-meant efforts can be questioned. Why does Mo Ibrahim (and other monied Africans like him) not use his money to support African thinkers, writers, and scientists; that is, have an African Nobel, rather than give this money to African leaders who are at the very heart of Africa's contemporary problems? Why does Africa's rich not use their money to support African publishing to get books written by Africans to African schools? The answer is, of course, it is their money. And I respect that; it is their money. Of course, Mo Ibrahim, in particular, is already doing a great job as a philanthropist--- we need more like him to perhaps follow that path and to fill the void in other areas.

I will miss Achebe because his passing away is concerning. Achebe was an able spokesperson for Africa and he did so with an unrivaled moral authority. On June 17, 1998, we invited him to give a James D. Wolfensohn Presidential Lecture at the World

Bank. Before his invitation, Nigeria's former finance minister, Ngozi Okonjo-Iweala, who was then a director in the World Bank, and I conspired to make the case that Achebe be invited. Initially, the Pakistani Tariq Hussain, who was then in charge of the Presidential Lecture series, was ambivalent, wondering how a writer might fare in an environment of hard-nosed bankers. Achebe proved him wrong and vindicated us. He came and gave a lecture titled, "Africa Is People," and the room was packed to standing room capacity. Even President Wolfensohn, so amazed by the attendance, quipped, "With this, maybe you should be president." And Achebe gave a brilliant speech. He argued for cancellation of debt owed by the poorest countries. He also argued for the World Bank to convince commercial institutions of the developed world to return stolen wealth stashed away by corrupt leaders from developing countries. He cited Wolfensohn's statistic, "You will be staggered to know, as I was, that 37 percent of African private wealth is held outside of Africa, whereas for Asia, the share is 3 percent, and for Latin America, it is 17 percent."[10] Achebe went on to note: "It would be a great pity if the world were to sit back in the face of this tragedy and do nothing, merely to preserve codes of banking etiquette and confidentially formulated for quite other times."[11] Achebe was making a revolutionary plea, and Wolfensohn sympathized with the message, and indeed did take heed later to champion a debt cancellation/forgiveness initiative known as the Highly Indebted Poor Countries (HIPC) initiative and also the World Bank Stolen Asset Recovery Initiative (STAR), from which many African countries benefited.

Achebe was a man of integrity. I will give one anecdote which startled me. In 1996, the Indian economist Ajay Chhibber, was leading a team of World Bank economists to produce the 1997 World Development Report (WDR), titled, *The State in a Changing World*. The WD report is the most important publication issued annually by the World Bank. Chhibber, knowing my connections with Achebe, asked me to approach him to write a paragraph on his thoughts about the "state" in Africa. Chhibber had read Achebe's *The Trouble with Nigeria*, and was impressed by its self-indicting, sober wisdom. Chhibber promised to pay $5,000 for the paragraph. I took up the mission and approached Achebe tactfully--- first, explaining the WDR and second, making the request. Achebe responded, in his usual polite, but frank manner: "Well, thank you for thinking about me. Sometimes you have to learn to say—no. Aha.... But thank you for thinking about me...." I conveyed the response to Chhibber, but reflected that this was a man who believed in his word. He was not ready to sell it for the quick buck. Also, in many a conversation with Achebe on the phone about publishing, he would despairingly comment, "publishing has been taken over by bookkeepers." He felt that over obsession with what sells has taken many a publishing house on the wrong path of not taking up valuable material, but material that would generate the quick buck. He would nostalgically recount his early days with Heinemann when publishers took interest in both the writer and the work.

 I will miss Achebe because his passing away is depriving and sad. His life was a consequential life--- it deeply touched many--- and offended few. I have tried in this essay not to rehash too much of the existing literature on Achebe for his writings have spawned an entire industry. I have tried, instead, only to recount a few memorable anecdotes and encounters

 I will miss Achebe--- our brother, our teacher. My feeling about his passing are best described in the following verse titled "Elegy for Chinua Achebe." May the wisdom he has left us be the pillow of peace on which his soul rests.

> Dear teacher, as we ponder your Exit,
> We know a weighty star in our sky has left us.
> Our bruised hopes seek your soaring light,
> At the edge of clouds. We stare. We mourn.
>
> Dear teacher, it cannot be the same.
> You were the luminous light from Ogidi.
> We drew to you because we believed your lore.
> In this, our twilight of loss, that Fate,
> So cruel, stole you, when unexpected.

We will remember you for your dreams to make Africa fly.
Your light to illuminate the untruths about Africa.
We will remember your integrity and your spine.

Now that you are suddenly gone, dear brother,
Who will tell us where the rain began to beat us?
Who will give us cultural hope to overcome our impediments?

Dear teacher, now that we have lost you,
Someone else must bear your weight.
And, now, as we ponder your Exit,
A heavy sadness squats in our hearts.
We will not let it go--
Until Africa awakes to your wisdom.

Notes

1 Amos Tutuola, *The Palm-Wine Drinkard* (New York: Grove Press, 1953), blurb.
2 Ernest Emenyonu, *The Rise of the Igbo Novel* (Ibadan: Ibadan University Press, 1987), 33.
3 Chinweizu, Onwuchekwa Jemie, and Ihechukwu Madubuike, *Toward the Decolonization of African Literature* (Washington, DC: Howard University Press, 1983), 288-89.
4 Chinua Achebe, *Things Fall Apart* (London: Heinemann Educational Books, 1967), 187.
5 Achebe, "Literature and Peace" *Lecture for the 2002 German Peace Prize* (Frankfurt am Main im Verlag: Borsenverein des Deutschen Buchhandels e.V., 13 October 2002), 42.
6 Hugh Trevor-Roper, *The Rise of Christian Europe* (London: Thames and Hudson, 1978), 9.
7 Ibid.
8 Tijan M. Sallah and Ngozi Okonjo-Iweala, *Chinua Achebe: Teacher of Light* (Trenton, NJ: Africa World Press, 2003), 105.
9 Achebe, "Publisher's Editorial," *African Commentary: A Journal of People of African Descent* 2, issues 1&2 (January/February 1990), 40.
10 Achebe, "Africa Is People," *Presidential Fellow Lecture Series* (Washington, DC: World Bank Institute, 1998), 8.
11 Ibid.

GLOSSARY

Aaat: in Wolof refers to uncircumcised boys.
Arigawo: refers to the Jola storyteller.
Assempulao: special helpers at Jola funerals who are usually the nieces or nephews of the dead person. They are given wide latitude to entertain guests.
Att: Wolof reference to the year.
Alek: in Wolof refers to tomorrow.
Assegai: a Southern African slim, iron-tipped spear with a wooden handle.
Badola: Wolof peasant or poor person.
Baakh: in Wolof means goodness.
Baaku: Wolof praise challenge poetry used in competitions like war or wrestling contests.
Baat: in Wolof means voice.
Bes bi: Wolof reference to the day.
Botal mbaar: in Wolof refers to the big brother or custodian of the shelter of the newly circumcised.
Bugaraab or Bukarabu: a Jola community dance festival which may last for up to six hours in one day in which three drums of different sizes are played.
Bunansanab: Jola funeral verse.
Burr: Wolof king.
Cham: in Wolof a praise challenge exclamatory device.
Daymba: in Wolof refers to yesterday.
Deey: in Wolof refers to death.
Dega: in Wolof means truth or truth telling.
Denku: an onomatopoeia referring to the rhythm of a wrestling match drum.

Deret: in Wolof refers to blood.
Derr: in Wolof refers to skin.
Dogh: in Wolof refers to a person walking.
Diwteer: palmoil used for cooking.
Djigum: in Jola, their women fertility shrine dance.
Dundah: in Wolof means life.
Ebunee: in Jola, their women retreat held annually to work on a particular topic during which a ceremonial queen is elected who serves at most for two years but has no royal powers.
Ekumpai: a Jola masked dancer draped in dried palm fronds like a spruce, with a sharp projectile protruding from its head.
Emitai: Jola supreme deity.
Emitai dabognol: Jola prophets or messengers of God.
Etta kat: Wolof caste of wood carvers.
Faida: in Wolof means being self-willing and self-directing.
Fank: the lowest level of decision-making in Jola society.
Fan werr: Wolof reference to the days of the moon or a month.
Fit: in Wolof refers to courage.
Fufu: pounded or mashed yam or cassava staple.
Fula: in Wolof means pride or dignified self-consciousness.
Futampaf: is a Jola rite of passage to adulthood initiation ceremony for young men between fifteen and thirty.
Gerr: member of Wolof caste of nobility.
Gerte saaf: roasted peanuts.
Gewel: member of the Wolof caste of musicians.
Gorr: Wolof free person with usufruct rights.
Guddi: Wolof reference to night.
Habaan mbaar: in Wolof refers to the oldest of the newly circumcised.
Ham ham: in Wolof means knowledge.
Houssahara: the Jola shrine for rain devoted to Aline Sitoe Jatta.
Huasene: refers to Jola ritual.
Jamano: inWolof refers to large chunks of time or to generational time.
Jambur: Wolof freeborn.
Jankha: in Wolof refers to a young adult girl.

Jom: in Wolof means dignity or integrity.
Judu: in Wolof refers to birth.
Kamambay: a much, derided smell in The Gambia coming from sweaty leather shoes.
Kankurang: a Jola masked dancer draped with the red bark of a tree and holding a cutlass; similar masked dancers also are used by the Mandinka. It is possible the Jola borrowed this dance ritual from them.
Kasila: a Jola community ritual seeking rain from God.
Kassak: Wolof circumcision poetry or song.
Katchikali: a crocodile shrine in Bakau, Kombo St. Mary Division, The Gambia.
Kebetu: Wolof rap poetry.
Kechimak: refers to Jola poetry.
Kerigeg (plural is Uregawu): refers to a Jola story.
Kersa: in Wolof means respectable predisposition towards others or being well-behaved.
Ki nu-y taga: Wolof praise recipient.
Kontaan: in Wolof refers to happiness.
Kuliye: a Jola naming ceremony held on the eight day after a child is born.
Kumakh Mbaar: in Wolof the spiritual protector of the shelter of newly circumcised.
Lamba: in Wolof refers to a wrestling match or a competitive process where the opponents are locked into feeling out each other's strengths.
Leb: Wolof story.
Lebaatu: Wolof proverb.
Linger: Wolof queen or princess.
Listiharr: a form of ritual seclusion to be with God to seek his help (from Arabic *salat-l-istikhara* or prayer for decision-making or for God's consent).
Lirr: in Wolof is a baby.
Makk: in Wolof refers to an adult.
Man man: in Wolof means ability or personal skill or what one is able to bear.
Mansali: refers to Jola proverbs.

Mbaar: in Wolof refers to the shelter for the newly circumcised; literarily means a "processing shop" where children are turned into young adults.

Moun: in Wolof means patience.

Nahaaru: in Wolof refers to pain or sadness.

Ndanaan: in Wolof refers to champion.

Naira: Nigerian currency.

Ndonki ndong: Wolof lead drum.

Nguneh: in Wolof refers to a toddler.

Nyenyo or Neno: a broad term for the lower castes of the Wolof constituted into various artisanal trades.

Ngamaan mbaar: in Wolof is the doctor to the newly circumcised.

Ngom: in Wolof refers to belief in oneself or in others.

Ngonn: Wolof reference to evening.

Nit: a Wolof reference to a human.

Njuli: in Wolof refers to the newly circumcised.

Nyakul: a Jola funeral dance done by men which involves ancestral songs.

Nyambeh ak nyebeh: boiled cassava and tomato stewed beans, a popular Gambian dish.

Nyambuwe: a Jola small naming ceremony, slightly less lavish as a *Kuliye*.

Passin: in Wolof refers to secret circumcision riddles to teach the newly circumcised adult secrets.

Piti: a Fula acrobatic dancer.

Raam: in Wolof refers to the crawling stage of humans.

Reeti: a Fula violin.

Raba kat: Wolof caste of weavers.

Rafet: in Wolof means beauty or beautiful.

Saa fara: in Wolof refers to protective magic potions.

Saani: in Wolof means to throw something.

Sagoe: in Wolof refers to self-regulating spirit or self conciousness.

Salbeh: in Wolof the guardians or assistants in a shelter of newly circumcised.

Samai: a Jola masked dancer who is dressed with discarded gunny sacks.
Sedet: in Wolof refers to muscle.
Sett: in Wolof means cleanliness.
Suba: Wolof reference to morning.
Taga: Wolof praise poetry.
Taga kat: Wolof praise singer.
Tahaaw: in Wolof refers to a person standing.
Takusaan: Wolof reference to afternoon.
Tega: Wolof caste of metal workers (goldsmiths, silver smiths, base metal workers).
Tegin: in Wolof refers to good manners.
Terranga: in Wolof means hospitality or being welcoming to strangers.
Terre: in Wolof means juju or protective amulets.
Teye: in Wolof refers to today.
Timis: Wolof reference to the onset of night.
Tohal mbaar: in Wolof refers to the youngest among the newly circumcised.
Ude: Wolof caste of leatherworkers.
Wahambaaneh: in Wolof refers to a young adult boy.
Wakh: in Wolof refers to speech.
Woi: in Wolof, a song.
Yaatu kai: Wolof reference to space; also "*diggante*" and "*jawu*" are use for space.
Yagh: in Wolof refers to one's bones.
Yapah: in Wolof refers to flesh.
Yaram: in Wolof refers to body.
Yarru: in Wolof means discipline.
Yurr: in Wolof refers to brain.

BIBLIOGRAPHY

Achebe, Chinua. *Africa is People*. Presidential Lecture Series, Washington, D.C.: World Bank Institute, 1998.
———. *Anthills of the Savannah*. New York: Anchor Books, 1988.
———. "Literature and Peace," *Lecture for the 2002 German Peace Prize*, Frankfurt am Main im Verlag: Borsenverein des Deutschen Buchhandels e.V., 13 October 2002.
———. *The Trouble with Nigeria*. Enugu, Nigeria: Fourth Dimension Publishing, 1983.
———. *Things Fall Apart*. New York: Fawcett Crest Books, 1969.
Arko, Kwame. "Protean Thou Shalt Be—Profile," *West Africa 23*, December-January 5, 1997.
Bamikunle, Aderemi. "Literature as a Historical Process: A Study of Ojaide's Labyrinths of the Delta," in *African Literature and African Historical Experience*, eds., Chidi Ikonne, Emelia Oko, and Peter Onwudinjo. Ibadan: Heinemann Nigeria, 1992.
Baum, Richard M. *West Africa's Women of God*. Bloomington: Indiana University Press, 2016.
Bloom, Harold, ed. *Langston Hughes: Bloom's Modern Critical Views*. New York: Chelsea Publishers, 1989.
Brown, Stewart. "Gambia Fictions," *Wasafiri*, Spring 1992, no. 15.
Camus, Albert. *The Rebel*. New York: Alfred A. Knopf, 1956.
Chinweizu. *The West and the Rest of Us*. Lagos, Nigeria: Pero Press, 1987.

_____, Onwuchekwa Jemie, and Ihechukwu Maduibike. *Toward the Decolonization of African Literature*. Washington, D.C.: Howard University Press, 1983.

Delafosse, Maurice. *Negroes of Africa*. Washington, D.C.: The Associated Publishers, 1931.

Dibba, Ebou. *Chaff in the Wind*. London: Macmillan Publishers, 1986.

Diop, Cheikh Anta. *Precolonial Black Africa*. West Port: Lawrence Hill & Company, 1987.

_____. *The African Origin of Civilization—Myth or Reality*. West Port: Lawrence Hill, 1974.

Du Bois, W.E.B. *The Souls of Black Folk*. Nashville: The Fisk University Press, 1979.

Egudu, Romanus. *Four West African Poets*. New York: Nok, 1977.

Ellison, Ralph. *Shadow and Act*. New York: Random House, 1994.

Emenyonu, Ernest. *The Rise of the Igbo Novel*. Ibadan: Ibadan University Press, 1987.

Franklin, John Hope and Alfred A. Moss, Jr. *From Slavery to Freedom, Sixth Edition*. New York: McGraw Hill Publishing, 1988.

Gailey, Harry. *Historical Dictionary of The Gambia*. New Jersey: The Scarecrow Press, 1975.

Gamble, David P. "Elementary Wolof Grammar," Brisbane, California: Gambian Studies, no. 25, unpublished, 1991, pp. 84-85.

Gamble, David P., Linda K. Salmon, and Alhaji Hassan Njie. *Peoples of the Gambia, vol. 1, The Wolof*. San Francisco: D.P. Gamble's Gambian Studies Series, no. 17, 1985.

Gardner, Helen, ed. *The New Oxford Book of English Verse*. Oxford: Oxford University Press, 1990.

Gates, Jr., H.L. *Figures in Black: Words, Signs and the "Racial" Self*. New York: Oxford University Press, 1987.

Haley, Alex. *The Autobiography of Malcolm X as Told to Alex Haley*. New York: The Ballantine Publishing Group, 1999.

Hansen, Marcus Lee. *The Problem of the Third Generation Immigrant*. Illinois: Augustana Historical Society, 1938.

Imfeld, Al. *Portraits of African Writers: Lenrie Peters, Horizon 1979 First Festival of World Culture*. Bonn: Deutsche Welle, 1979.

Isani, Muktar Ali Isani. "'Gambia on My Soul': Africa and the African in the Writings of Phillis Wheately," *Melus*, 6, Spring 1979.

Jahateh, Lamin. "Recovery of Jammeh's 'Stolen Assets' Would Take Years," Banjul, The Gambia: *The Point*, July 14, 2017.

Larson, Charles. *The Emergence of African Fiction*. Bloomington: Indiana University Press, 1972.

Locke, Alain, ed. *The New Negro, Voices of the Harlem Renaissance*. New York: Simon & Shuster, 1997.

Ojaide, Tanure. *Eagle's Vision*. Michigan: Lotus Press, 1987.

_____. *The Endless Song*. Lagos, Nigeria: Malthouse Press, 1989.

_____. *Labyrinths of the Delta*. New York: The Greenfield Review, 1990.

_____. "The Changing Voice of History: Contemporary African Poetry," *Geneve-Afrique*, 27, no. 1, 1989.

_____. *The Fate of Vultures and Other Poems*. Lagos, Nigeria: Malthouse Press, 1990.

Padmore, George, ed. *History of Pan African Congress*. London: The Hammersmith Bookshop, 1963.

Mahoney, Florence. *The Liberated Slaves and The Question of the Return to Africa: From the Slave Trade to the Challenge of Development*. Kanifing, The Gambia: Book Production and Material Resources Unit, 2001.

McKay, Claude. *Harlem Shadows: The Poems of Claude McKay*. New York: Harcourt, Brace and Company, 1922.

Morris, Johnson et. al. *From Freedom to African Roots in American Soil*. New York: Random House, 1977.

Peters, Lenrie. *The Second Round*. London: Heinemann Educational Books, 1979.

_____. *Selected Poetry*. London: Heinemann Educational Books, 1981.

Perfect, David. *Historical Dictionary of The Gambia, Fifth Edition*. Lanham: Rowman and Littlefield, 2016.

Perry, Margaret. *Silence to the Drums: A Survey of the Literature of the Harlem Renaissance*. West Port: Greenwood Press, 1976.

Quarles, Benjamin. *The Negro in the Making of America*. New York: Touchstone, 1987.

Randall, Dudley, ed. *The Black Poets: An Anthology*. New York: Bantam Book, 1971.

Reeve, Henry Fenwick. *The Gambia: Its History, Ancient, Medieval and Modern*. New York: Negro Universities Press, 1969.

Reid, Stuart A. "The Dictators Who Love America," *The Atlantic*, February 8, 2016.

Roberts, Pamela. *Black Oxford: The Untold Stories of Oxford University's Black Scholars*. Oxford: Signal Books, 2013.

Saine, Abdoulaye. *The Paradox of Third-wave Democratization in Africa*. Lanham, MD: Lexington Books, 2009.

Sallah, Tijan. *Koraland*. Washington, D.C.: Three Continents Press, 1989.

_____. *Wolof*. New York: The Rosen Publishing Group, 1996.

_____. "Words or Rice? The State of Literature in The Gambia," *Daily Observer*, October 8, 1993.

_____. and Ngozi Okonjo-Iweala. *Chinua Achebe: Teacher of Light*. Trenton, NJ: Africa World Press, 2003.

Sapir, J. David. *A Grammar of Diola-Fogny*. Cambridge: Cambridge University Press, 1965.

_____. Website, *Kujamaat Language and Folk Materials*. Charlottesville: University of Virginia, Anthropology Department.

Schwarz-Bart, Simone. *In Praise of Black Women*. Madison: The University of Wisconsin Press, 2003.

Soyinka, Wole. "Culture, Memory, and Development," Keynote Address in *Culture and Development in Africa*, eds. Ismail Serageldin and June Taboroff, Washington, D.C.: The World Bank, 1992.

Trevor-Roper, Hugh. *The Rise of Christian Europe*. London: Thames and Hudson, 1978.

Tutuola, Amos. *The Palm-Wine Drinkard*. New York: Grove Press, 1953.

Unknown Senegalese Author. "Tradition and Cultural Identity in Senegal," Unpublished paper, 1991.

Wagner, Jean. *Black Poets of the United States: From Paul Laurence Dunbar to Langston Hughes*. Urbana: University of Illinois Press, 1973.

Waweru, Nduta. "Meet Pierre Atepa Goudiaby, The Senegalese Architect Behind the Most Prolific Landmarks in Africa," *Face2Face Africa*, September 3, 2018.

Wheatley, Phillis. *Poems on Various Subjects, Religious and Moral*. Philadelphia: Joseph Crukshank, 1786.

Wyse, Akintola. *The Krio of Sierra Leone: An Interpretive History*. Washington, D.C.: Howard University Press, 1991.

INDEX

A

Achebe, Chinua · vii, ix, xiii, 4, 11, 20, 22, 30, 37, 151, 154, 157, 159, 163, 167, 169, 170
Achebe, Ikechukwu · 166
African Commentary · 165, 166, 170

B

Barrow, Adama · 89
Baum, Robert M. · 77
Brown, Stewart · 13, 16, 22

C

Camus, Albert · 135, 142
Carruth, Hayden · 144
Casamance · 3, 65, 66, 70, 77, 78, 79, 81, 82, 83, 85, 87
Cham, Mbye · 15, 107
Charles, Prince · 93
Chhibber, Ajay. 168, 169.
Chinweizu · 117, 124, 160, 165, 170
Churchill, Winston · 133, 134
Conarteh, Swaebou · 13, 16
Cullen, Countee · 132, 138

D

Dibba, Ebou · 13, 15, 16, 17, 18, 20, 22, 89, 103
Diop, Cheikh Anta · 24, 28, 37, 116, 124
Du Bois, W. E. B. · 5, 126, 127, 128, 129, 141

F

Faal, Kochy Barma · 61, 64
Feloups · 66
Fula · 1, 17, 30, 31, 172, 175

G

Gambia, The · xiii, 1, 2, 3, 4, 5, 6, 7, 9, 10, 11, 12, 13, 14, 15, 16, 17, 18, 20, 21, 22, 23, 37, 39, 42, 48, 65, 66, 67, 68, 70, 71, 84, 85, 86, 87, 88, 89, 90, 91, 93, 97,

99, 100, 101, 102, 103, 104, 105, 107, 108, 109, 110, 111, 117, 118, 119, 124, 167, 173
Gamble, David P. · 27, 31, 32, 36, 37, 63, 64
Garren, Samuel · 15
Garvey, Marcus A. · 5, 126, 127
Gates Jr., Henry Louis · 113, 124
Goudiaby Atepa, Pierre · 85, 87

H

Harlem · vii, xii, 125, 126, 128, 129, 130, 132, 137, 138, 140, 141, 142
Harlem Renaissance · vii, xii, 125, 126, 128, 130, 138, 140, 141, 142
Harvard University · 138
Hebrew · 122
Hughes, Langston · 132, 137, 138, 139, 140, 141, 142, 153

I

Ibrahim, Mo. 167

J

Jagne, Siga · 15
Jammeh, Yahya · 65, 85, 86, 87, 88, 89

Jatta, Aline Sitoe · 66, 77, 87, 173
Jawara, Sir Dawda · 15, 85, 92, 93, 100
Jola · vii, xi, xii, 1, 3, 16, 17, 31, 65, 66, 67, 68, 69, 70, 71, 72, 73, 74, 75, 76, 77, 78, 79, 80, 81, 82, 83, 84, 85, 86, 87, 93, 171, 172, 173, 174, 175

K

Khan, Mariama · ix, 15, 90, 91
Kibre Negest · 162
Kolley, Momodou · 84, 87
Kombo St. Mary · 173
Krio · 4, 12, 13, 16, 20, 21, 100, 102

L

Langley, Jabez Ayodele · 15
Locke, Alain · 130, 131, 132, 136, 140, 141, 142

M

Mahfouz, Naguib · 164
Mahoney, Florence (née Peters) · 5, 100, 101, 102, 110
Mali · 77, 82, 162
Mandinka · 1, 16, 17, 71, 91, 95, 173
Maxwell, Joseph Renner · 101, 102, 165

McKay, Claude.
132,133,134,135,136,137
Moore, Francis · 21, 67, 68, 87, 145

N

NAACP · 128, 129
Ndanaan · 12, 13, 14, 89, 174
Ndibe, Okey · 165
Negro · xii, 87, 101, 113, 115, 119, 120, 121, 122, 125, 126, 127, 128, 129, 130, 131, 132, 134, 136, 137, 140, 141, 142
New Negro · 125, 130, 131, 138, 140, 141, 142
Niasse, Cheikh Ibrahima · 19
Nkrumah, Kwame · 19, 165
Nnaji, Bartholomew · 165
Nyang, Sulayman S. · 17, 37, 42

O

Obiechina, Emmanuel · 163
Ohaeto, Ezenwa · 15
Ojaide, Tanure · vii, ix, xii, 143, 144, 145, 146, 147, 148, 149, 150, 151, 152, 153, 154, 155, 156, 157
Okonjo-Iweala, Ngozi · 168, 170
Olubunmi Smith, Pamela J. 15.
Owomoyela, Onyekan. 107.
Oxford University · 5, 21, 101, 110, 124, 130

P

Peters, Lenrie · vii, xii, xiii, 3, 4, 5, 21, 90, 93, 97, 99, 100, 103, 105, 110
Plessy vs. Ferguson · 127
Pushkin, Alexsandr · 116

R

Reeve, Henry Fenwick · 68, 69, 70, 87
Roberts, Gabriel · 97
Roper, Hugh-Trevor · 162, 163, 170

S

Saho, Bala · ix, 95, 96
Sall, Amadou Lamine · 91
Sallah, Momodou · ix, 84, 87, 90, 93, 97
Sallah, Tijan M. · xiii, 13, 15, 16, 21, 64, 170
Sarr, Sheriff · 13, 16
Senegal · 1, 3, 13, 17, 19, 23, 25, 31, 37, 39, 42, 61, 64, 65, 66, 77, 82, 83, 84, 85, 87, 99, 106, 167
Senegambia · vii, xi, 17, 23, 27, 39, 65, 111, 112
Senghor, Leopold Sedar · 10, 11, 81, 109
Shaarawi, Amr · 164
Shaarawi, Huda · 164
Shagari, Shehu · 146, 147
Shaka · 156
Singhateh, Sally · 16, 89

Slavery · 121, 140, 141, 142
Soyinka, Wole · xii, 104, 143, 144, 147, 156, 157

T

Thomas, Dylan · 159
Timbuktu · 77, 82, 162
Tukulor · 91, 92, 93
Tutuola, Amos · 159, 170

W

Washington, Booker T. · 126
Wheatley, Phillis · vii, ix, xii, 111, 112, 114, 116, 118, 121, 122, 123, 124, 129

Wolfensohn, James D. · 168
Wolof · vii, xi, 1, 13, 16, 17, 18, 19, 23, 24, 25, 26, 27, 28, 29, 31, 32, 33, 36, 37, 39, 40, 41, 43, 44, 45, 46, 47, 48, 49, 50, 51, 52, 53, 60, 61, 63, 64, 90, 91, 92, 93, 95, 105, 162, 167, 171, 172, 173, 174, 175, 176
Woodson, Carter G. · 129
Wyse, Akintola · 4, 21

X

X, Malcolm · 127, 140, 141, 180